Positively Speaking

The Art of
Constructive Conversations
with a Solutions Focus

by

Paul Z Jackson and

Janine Waldman

First published in the United Kingdom in 2010 by The Solutions Focus
Second edition 2011

© Paul Z Jackson, Janine Waldman

British Library Cataloguing-in-Publication Data
A catalogue record for this book is available from the British Library.

Printed in the United Kingdom

Introduction to Positively Speaking: The Art of Constructive Conversations with a Solutions Focus

This book is aimed at building your skills, so you can enjoy better results from your conversations. It takes you step by step through practical exercises, supported by tips, stories and examples.

We take a solution-focused (SF) perspective, and of course much has been written about the philosophy of SF and even more about its therapeutic applications. But until now, there has been too little about how to get more of what you want in conversations at work; during informal coaching dialogues; in instant performance management; by meeting a colleague for a quick talk by the water-cooler. All of these provide opportunities for the constructive conversationalist to achieve so much more.

Over the years we have introduced wide-ranging change programmes in organisations, run many training courses and written books and articles. We now think that conversation is the fundamental unit of change. It is conversation by conversation where the application of SF skills makes the biggest differences.

When we present coaching clinics or review sessions to find out how budding solutionists are getting on, the questions are predominantly about face-to-face interactions. Here – and one-to-one on the telephone – are where the skills matter. And this study guide is about developing those skills in those contexts.

Skill building typically takes time and often feels unnatural at first. New skills become habitual when you really want them, and the process is eased if you are rewarded with small successes along the way. By practicing the techniques on offer in this book, you will start to experience better results at work, better relationships and clearer communications straight away. As you develop your abilities, you can find yourself doing less work that you don't want, while those around you take on more of what they should be doing. You'll lose any fears of awkward and difficult conversations and instead will look forward to making progress with the more or less willing collaboration of others.

Even experienced SF practitioners will find new approaches and insights here, yet all the tools have been tried and tested in the most demanding of circumstances.

The course is structured and presented as a six-week program. That is fine if it suits you, but you don't have to take it literally. Go at your own pace, bearing in mind that you'll gain the greatest benefits if you do take the time to practice what you are learning, in real circumstances with real people, who don't know you are experimenting. You are invited to create a personal laboratory – which can be fun and illuminating, as well as generating amazing break-throughs. Not everything has to work first time – apply these powerful ideas with a responsive and adaptive frame of mind to build confidence and increase your impact.

In Week One, you are introduced to the notion of constructive conversations and decide where you might apply the concepts. You learn the crucial distinction between Problem talk and Solutions Talk, against a background of the six SF principles. In the next chapter, you will discover great ways to begin a constructive conversation – including methods for negotiating a solid platform with your dialogue partners on which to build an inspiring vision of a desired future.

Chapter 3 reveals the central importance of discussing what's already working, describing the collecting of 'counters' and several variations of scaling to enable us to notice, measure and achieve progress. We also look in detail at the subtle possibilities of 'presuppositional language.'

We get to grips with the pragmatics of making things happen in Chapter 4, with the motivational power of affirming and the commitment to action of decisive small steps.

At around the half way point, there's time out to reflect on the extent to which you are getting what you want. As you apply all the tools, you may want to scale up your ambition and tackle even tougher cases. These are explored in more detail in Week 5, with a range of complete examples from various contexts – including those crucial performance management conversations. By now, you'll be ready to develop your own spins on constructive conversations, aided by our guide to JAM (just-a-minute) Sessions.

In the final chapter we take a more detailed look at how these tools and techniques fit within the intellectual landscape and reflect with you on the progress you'll have made and the progress still to come.

Whether it is with our clients, our colleagues, our bosses; or with our families and friends, we want to get the best out of our conversations. Now it's time for you to dip into this guide and use these simple, proven tools to hold more effective conversations and get yourself the outstanding results that you want.

We have learnt much from talking with our clients, colleagues and mentors. We offer huge thanks to them all, including Steve de Shazer and Insoo Kim Berg; our trainers at Brief; the many inspiring solutionists at EBTA, SOL and UKASFP events. Thanks too to Robert Biswas-Diener and his colleagues at CAPP for prompting us to get this book written. There's also a lifetime of conversation and dialogue ahead, and we welcome your feedback, comments and questions. Positively.

Paul Z Jackson and Janine Waldman, 2010, contact@thesolutionsfocus.co.uk

Table of Contents

Week 1: Introducing your changing conversations

Welcome to *Positively Speaking*: *The Art of Constructive Conversations with a Solutions Focus*. In this first chapter we'll be exploring what makes some conversations better than others, and outlining the solutions-focused approach - the tools and principles that will enable you to hold more constructive conversations every time you choose to speak.

We'll also be finding out what you are already doing that's working – more than you may imagine - and what you want from participating in this course.

Constructive conversations are about getting what you want, professionally and personally, by engaging in skilled communications with those around you.

There are many ways to have a conversation. If you reflect on your recent conversations, you might find some were energised, informative, enjoyable and made progress, whilst others were difficult, draining, full of misunderstanding or just plain dull.

We imagine that you would rather be having the first kind of conversations – constructive conversations. Solutions Focus, a positive approach to change, offers you tools, principles and applications that you can simply apply to enjoy more constructive conversations more of the time – whether it's with your clients, boss, colleagues, partner, friends or family.

As we work together through this guide, you'll have the opportunity to absorb the theory and apply the tools to situations of your choice.

Constructive conversations – and getting what you want

Let's explore further what we mean by the term 'constructive conversation'. A constructive conversation is any conversation in which you make progress. If you change the conversation, then there's every chance you'll change everything that surrounds it - your relationships with colleagues, how you get on with your family and friends, your very ability to accomplish whatever you want.

Those may seem big claims for the humble conversation, but if we appreciate the centrality of dialogue to human communication, and communication as the engine of our interactions, then we begin to see the power of making more of what's available to us - whenever we open our mouths.

And you'll not be alone in taking this route. Ideally, you make progress by developing it in dialogue with the other person (or people) involved. In that sense it is co-constructed - built by both parties, as you go along. It's having the conversations that makes the difference.

There is a difference after the conversation is over, and it was constructive if things are somehow better than they were before. Now, perhaps, one or more people are clearer about what to do. Or the relationship between them has improved so that they are more prepared to tackle the next challenge.

We have all had many constructive conversations. You couldn't have got to where you are now without doing so. You could probably list hundreds of conversations that enabled you to get through school and college, find work, collaborate on projects, decide to which school to send your kids, learn who is and who isn't a friend, and many, many more.

We are social beings and it is our conversations with others that help determine our route through life. So all of us have plenty of raw research material to identify what makes a conversation constructive and we have the skills to carry out such conversations. However you may not yet have appreciated what knowledge and abilities you have.

You may not yet have found the vocabulary for discussing it or the models to make sense of it. Part of this program is to help you identify what works for you, what's worked for others, and to decide how you can apply these learnings from now on.

This will involve experimenting - trying things out to see what happens; and noticing what impacts your different strategies and tactics bring out - in yourself and in those with whom you are talking.

Every experiment will present an opportunity to improve your communication skills, hone your emotional intelligence and reap the rewards of decades of research into positive psychology.

You'll be applying cutting-edge solutions-focused tools to a wide range of professional and personal circumstances. For example, as well as having experienced constructive conversations, you'll probably have had difficult conversations from time to time.

You may have had trouble conveying simple information, you may have struggled to influence someone in the direction you want or failed to persuade others of your point of view. Perhaps there are times when you even have to deal with out-and-out conflict or opposed needs – and must do your best to prevent the situation from escalating, so you can resolve it with the best outcomes for the agreement (such as it is) and the relationships between the people involved. This program will equip you with strategies and tools to apply in these – and many other situations.

What will be the positive impacts of positively speaking for you?

Take a moment to imagine what will be better or different for you when you have reached the end of this program and have developed the skill to have even more constructive conversations than you do now:

○ What might you be doing?
○ What would be better?
○ What might others notice about you?
○ What would be the positive impact of this for you and those around you?

So, in that spirit, let's get started with the first exercises in this program - getting clearer about what you want from it.

Exercise 1.1
Building your Platform for the program

Please complete the following sentences, to record for yourself what will be useful reminders about your aims and objectives.

What I want from this course is....

The kinds of conversations in which I might be able to use the ideas from this guide include...

Some people with whom I'm looking forward to having more constructive conversations include...

Our aim and our approach

Whether it is with your clients, your colleagues, your bosses or even your families, our aim here is for you to get the best out of your conversations and minimise those difficulties.

What approaches are available to us? We can enter a conversation blindly and hope for the best. Or we can take a more strategic approach to discussions, planning how we want them to go and then be willing and skilled enough to adjust our tactics during the conversation itself. The latter turns out generally to be the better way to get more of what we want.

It's also important to note that none of the techniques in this approach are about convincing others you are correct, bullying them, or otherwise tricking people into letting you get you what you want at their expense.

Some simple tips can make all the difference – as long as you have the discipline to put them into practice. Most of us would probably agree that it's a good idea to remain polite and friendly, even in difficult circumstances, but do you have the strength of mind to stay that way in the face of rudeness or other provocations?

Are you confident in your ability to handle emotions safely – both yours and your conversation partners? If not, perhaps you could adopt some well-tried strategies to take pre-emptive steps - to stop the discussions becoming so difficult in the first place.

Let's create a benchmark for your current skills in holding constructive conversations.

Exercise 1.2
Benchmarking

Rate yourself on a scale of 1 (lowest) to 10 (highest) on each of the following:

I am consistently successful in persuading people what to do

I am good at handling my own strong emotions in conversations

I am good at handling other people's strong emotions during conversations

I prepare well for difficult conversations

I am good at staying polite when provoked.

Add some more statements that describe how you would like to be in relation to your constructive conversations – and then rate yourself against the scale.

You can come back to this checklist at the end of the program to assess your own progress.

Where the solution-focused approach comes from

Before we explore further the solutions-focused tools and principles that underpin constructive conversations, here's a brief summary of the origins of the approach.

Solutions Focus has its roots in the therapeutic approach devised by Insoo Kim Berg and Steve de Shazer in Milwaukee, Wisconsin (USA).

Working with therapy patients, they were seeking the most efficient ways of making progress. The traditional approach of 'the talking cure', deriving from Freud and psychoanalysis, involved months or even years of conversations, exploring the 'roots' of issues in childhood, uncovering traumas and – as the name implies – reaching an 'analysis' – that is a detailed understanding of the problem.

As the profession developed, family therapy offered help to family groups – the parents would attend sessions, say, with the 'difficult' child, based on the idea that the problems might be in the interactions between the family members. This more systemic approach built on the insights of social anthropologist Gregory Bateson.

De Shazer and Berg (and their colleagues) experimented with the types of questions they asked and the order in which they asked them, developing SFBT – solution focused brief therapy. One striking finding was that patients made better progress when they were asked about what they wanted (solutions) before (or – more radically - instead of) when they were asked about their problems.

Dealing, for example, with people who drank too much, they discovered that these people typically wanted something different in their lives, such as spending more time with their children or improving the quality of their marriage. By discussing with their patients what was wanted – which often seemed unrelated to the presenting problem – the therapists got results more quickly, and just as sustainably, as other therapeutic methods.

Following the philosopher Ludwig Wittgenstein, they proposed that there may be no logical connection between 'the problem' – what was troubling people – and 'the solution' – what people wanted. This was, and remains, a strikingly bold assertion. Yet, whether or not this was a satisfactory explanation for their success, Berg and de Shazer's model spread through parts of the therapy world, with excellent results documented by several research studies.

Their insights are now backed by a far wider and larger range of research from the fast-developing field of positive psychology. Positive psychology, popularized by American psychologist Martin Seligman, is the scientific study of happiness, strengths and why and how people flourish. This new field dovetails nicely with the inherently positive approach of solutions focus work.

Berg and de Shazer's solution-focused approach also began to find its way into organizations and businesses that saw benefits in a direct and pragmatic way of getting what people wanted. Many consultants, facilitators and managers now apply the approach and techniques to managing change, strategic planning, conflict resolution, leadership and coaching.

One of the authors of this study guide, Paul Z Jackson, played a significant part in this development, co-founding the network of solution-focus practitioners (SOLworld) and devising with Mark McKergow a set of tools and principles for working with a solution-focused approach in organisations. These are captured in their book "The Solutions Focus – making coaching and change SIMPLE".

We suggest you check out some of the resources on the web, such as SOLworld, UKASFP and EBTA, listed at the end of this chapter, to learn more about the many applications of a solution-focused approach.

Principles of a solutions-focused approach to constructive conversations

The main principles of a solutions-focused approach can help you deal more confidently and effectively with even the toughest of conversations.

These principles, forming the acronym SIMPLE, provide you with a comprehensive checklist to ensure your conversations will be as constructive as possible.

Solutions - not problems

Inbetween – not individual

Make Use of What's There – not what isn't

Possibilities – from the past, present and future

Language – Clear not complicated

Every case is different

Let's look at them in turn.

The first principle is to focus on **Solutions, not problems**. This is a notion to help you get what you want by keeping on track, not wasting time discussing what you don't want. For example, you might be a manager dealing with Andy, a member of staff who is consistently turning up late. Focusing the conversation on what you don't want – Andy turning up late – is likely to lead to accusatory-sounding questions such as "Why are you always late?", followed by denials, defensiveness or excuses, none of which get you any closer to your desires.

What you want is Andy turning up on time, so we suggest making that the focus of the conversation, with more constructive questions, such as "Andy, what has to happen for you to get here on time?" You can focus on solutions as part of your planning, by asking yourself in advance what it is you want from a conversation and by preparing questions and statements that will inject these terms into the discussion itself; "Let's talk about how we can ensure you get to work on time…. You arrived in good time three days last week – how did you achieve that?" You can maintain your focus on solutions during the conversation, by checking as it goes along that it is still about the desired aspects of the topic and not wandering into the dangerous and less helpful territories of what's not wanted and the dire consequences thereof.

The next principle is **Inbetween** – which reminds us that the action is in the interaction. It's not just about the other person and it's not just about you. It's about the interaction between the two of you, which stands a chance of changing things by the end of the conversation. For example, in conflicts, you both want something, and there's a good chance that you will get more of what you want if you acknowledge (at the very least) what your partner wants, and – better still – can go some way towards helping them get it, even if it may be partly at the expense of what you want. Plan in advance what you might be willing to give away, and make it clear during the conversation that you are interested in the other party's outcomes.

The Inbetween principle reminds you that your part of a conversation can be altered (from what you thought you might say) by what the other person says. And what you say will affect – moment to moment – what they say. This opens up possibilities, as we see overleaf.

One school receptionist told us during a workshop that many of the people who approached her desk or called her on the phone were miserable and rude. She said she felt the place was gloomy and realised that she was feeling gloomy too. Determined to make her reception area a happier place to spend her days, she started smiling at everybody as they entered the building, saying 'good morning', asking how their weekend had been and generally being more cheery. She also changed her telephone greeting by adding a friendly 'hello' before identifying the school. She noticed over time that visitors seemed to be happier; not only were they now smiling at her, they were smiling at each other. Callers too were friendlier, and the gloom she had been feeling had somehow lifted from the building.

Our third principle is **Make Use of What's There,** which means taking advantage of how matters actually are. If you can accept whatever it is you are facing, you are in a good position to utilise whatever that may be – in contrast, perhaps, to wishing it were different, or complaining about what's missing or not there.

A good starting point for Making Use of What's There is to be aware of your own resources for the conversations you are embarking upon: what do you have that counts usefully for you – a certain authority, statutory or titular rights, good reasons for what you want to propose, personal credibility, credit in your emotional bank account? How might these play their part in your constructive conversation?

Making Use of What's There also encourages you to improvise as the conversation develops, just as you might improvise a meal from whatever ingredients you found in your fridge if friends turned up unexpectedly.. You'll learn more later about the improvisational skills of listening, acknowledging and creative response, all of which will help you achieve more of what you want in conversations.

There's a terrific story of Making Use of What's There on a grand, political scale in Levitt and Dubner's book, *Freakonomics.*

During the post-World War II revival of the white supremacist Ku Klux Klan, a Southern gentleman by the name of Stetson Kennedy infiltrated the Klan with a view to destabilising it.

His most productive ploy was to feed the society's secret codes and passwords to the writers of the nightly 'Adventures of Superman' radio series. They included these in a four-week story in which Superman fought the Klan.

Suddenly, the Klan members were complaining that their children were ridiculing the Klan's catchphrases and costumes. Membership applications dried up, and the revival was over. As Levitt and Dunbar write, "It had the precise effect he hoped: turning the Klan's secrecy against itself, converting precious knowledge into ammunition for mockery."

By combining two resources at his disposal – the secret knowledge and his access to the radio show – Stetson got what he wanted to great effect.

We were working with a senior manager, Martin, whose organisation had just taken over another, smaller company, with the aim of making it more productive. Staff in the new acquisition had a reputation for taking long tea-breaks, a clear example of their 'lack of dynamism' – which presented both a problem and an opportunity.

Martin was worried about the different cultures and excessive breaks, so we asked him how he might make use of this. Thinking about how to make use of what was there, Martin came up with the idea of introducing himself to his new colleagues, and letting them know the ethos and expectations of the company they now found themselves part of – during the tea-breaks.

Suddenly the tea-breaks became a more productive part of the working day, and Martin's neat initiative allowed the staff to make the transition to the new ways of working far more seamless and painless than Martin or they had previously imagined.

P is for **Possibilities** – from the past, present and future. For possibilities from the past, you are encouraged to recall previously successful conversations, perhaps with this same person, perhaps on the same sort of topic with someone else. Maybe there are hints or inspirations there that can help you this time.

Future possibility is your sense that this conversation can go well – that you are approaching it with hope. Consider what it is that you hope for and what grounds you may have for optimism here.

Remember too the concept of the interactional world, which may invoke a feeling of flexibility and possibility in the present. It means you can reduce the assumptions in your head about how the conversation is going to go. You don't have to think, for example, that it is going to be difficult. Perhaps it won't be. Suppose, instead, that it goes well: how will you know; what will you be saying, what will they be saying?

The next principle is **Language – Clear not complicated.** Your conversations will be more constructive if you and other people involved understand what is going on. Using vocabulary that is as simple as possible, avoiding complicated words, phrases and jargon will help keep everyone on track.

Whenever possible, use the words spoken by the other person – speak their language. Sometimes you will need to paraphrase to check you have understood, or to summarise a long passage of speech. At other times, you'll benefit from using their exact words – this will indicate to the other person that you have been listening carefully and that they have been heard. We can suppose that they know what they mean by their words, so your interpretation is unlikely to be required or welcome.

We recall one conversation in which an engineer told us, "The problem is the supervisor's superiority complex with the N-types". We noted this word-for- word on the flipchart and asked, "What is it you want with the supervisor's superiority complex with the N-types?" He leapt with excitement and said, "Yes, I know exactly what to do. Brilliant," which appeared to end our conversation satisfactorily for him. To this day we still have no idea what was going on with the supervisor or the N-types.

The final principle is to appreciate how **Every case is different.** This brings a couple of distinct benefits. One is to remind you to remain alert to what is uniquely to your advantage in this situation. The other is to save you from applying tactics that may have worked before and being surprised that they don't work this time. For example, suppose you are trying to make a sale to a new customer. With previous sales, the critical factor has always been price – and you know you are willing to offer a discount to make the sale. Just before you play your familiar discount card, you suddenly realise that this time the discussion is all about some other aspect of the service – quality, perhaps, or speed of delivery – and by improvising alertly in the moment and going with the new flow of the conversation, you are able to increase your profit margin and still give the client everything that matters to them.

A handy question to ask yourself before or during a conversation – particularly one that may be problematic or tricky is, "What might I be able to do in this discussion that I've not done before?" Always look for the unique opportunity.

Exercise 1.3
Forthcoming conversations

Here's something to try during the week before the next module.

Take a moment to consider the significant conversations you are anticipating over the next few days. Select one or two to be your experimental test beds – perhaps those that you are most and least looking forward to.

Make a note here of these conversations:

How can you apply these principles to them?

If you can identify why you will be having these conversations at all, you can pick out what's in it for you – and how you can benefit if they go as well as they possibly can.

Prepare for that, allowing for the interactional elements of your partner putting forward their case, and for the possibility of it turning out just that little bit better than you are currently expecting.

Getting started with conflicting views

What if you want very different outcomes from the conversation than the other party?

When dealing with difficult conversations – whether during development discussions, conflicts or similar situations - one party often has strong views about the solution to be executed. But this may not be the best outcome for all the parties. It needs a good communicator, with a powerful set of tools, to lead the consultation to the best results.

It may well be useful to discover what the other person wants and needs, so that by going some way towards satisfying their needs, you put them in a position in which they may be more inclined to help you get what you want. By asking the right questions, you can construct a better joint solution in the discussion.

Problem Talk and Solutions Talk

If you want to have consistently constructive conversations, perhaps the most important distinction to grasp is that between Problem Talk and Solutions Talk. It is also the most subtle.

Problem Talk is – as the name implies – talk about problems: it includes descriptions of what the problems are, analysis of where they came from, elaboration of the effects they are having, how people feel about them, and speculation about what they are leading to. It is any talk that puts the focus on the Problem.

There is a great deal of Problem Talk in the world, which is not surprising because people experience many problems and naturally want to talk about them. They want to tell other people about their personal problems, probe into other folks' interesting problems, and discuss the problems of the world. Whether the problem is small or large, trivial or earth-shattering, people want to talk about it. They may even want to solve these problems and expect that the conversations about the problems are part of the problem-solving effort. There's an entire industry of problem-solving, with an extensive bookshelf of titles dedicated to the arts of solving problems – societal, industrial, team, familial, marital and individual.

And there is, of course, merit in problem-solving, when it is successful. And therefore there is merit in Problem Talk, if it's the sort that leads to solved problems, or if it leads to understanding (if that's what you want) or to have 'got something off your chest' (if that's what you want).

In fact, Problem Talk has had such a history of success, especially in analysis-driven professions such as medicine, engineering and all their derivatives, that it has become (for most people) an automatic way of talking and thinking about topics whenever something is not as satisfactory as it might be.

Yet it is possible that the value of Problem Talk is over-rated and that there may be a more useful way of discussing matters, particularly when problems persist and Problem Talk is failing to help us solve some of the more complex, knotty issues that people face. It's also worth considering that Problem Talk is making things worse. If we can have constructive conversations, it is also possible to have destructive conversations, where the talk leads to "stuckness" or further difficulties. Perhaps focusing on problems magnifies the perception of the problem, making people more miserable, more depressed, less optimistic and less resourceful.

An alternative means of discourse is Solutions Talk. Solutions Talk is talk about what is wanted: it includes descriptions of how matters will be when they are the way people want them to be, it includes talk of resources, strengths and skills, of successful examples, of actions that will help us to get to desired states of affairs.

We (the authors) have the feeling that we are on an historic cusp, where the mechanical view of the world that has served us so well for the past two hundred years can be usefully superseded by a complexity view of the world in which attending to systems and their dynamic interactions will produce better results. And that our conversations – the way we use our language and our thoughts – will need to adapt and catch up to make the most of this shift.

Let's consider some examples to ensure we have a good sense of the difference between Problem Talk and Solutions Talk, and then briefly note where this breakthrough distinction came from.

Meet the manager, the coach and the parent

The manager

We met Hans Zeinhofer at a conference where delegates were discussing the application of solutions-focused ideas in organisations. Hans was the general manager of a power supply company in Austria, and he described the crisis they had faced when a confusing letter was sent to all their customers, which many interpreted to mean they would be cut off from their supply. The letter prompted thousands of calls and complaints from customers, overwhelming the switchboards and customer care department.

Somehow they got through the crisis and two weeks later Hans convened the meeting of his managers to discuss what had happened.

The expected topic for this meeting was 'to discuss the reasons for this incredible disaster'. In such a meeting, managers would explore how the letter got out there – perhaps identifying who wrote it, where they had gathered their misinformation, who had authorised it and who failed to prevent it. Then they would explore the weaknesses of the switchboard and other response mechanisms. There would probably be several people to blame, departments accusing each other of various failings – and perhaps eventually measures proposed to stop such a letter ever being issued again.

It was, therefore, a meeting that the managers were not looking forward to with any degree of pleasure.

But Hans had recently attended a training course in the Solutions Focus approach and decided – "very nervously" – to put his new learnings into practice. He went into the meeting, he told us, and put these questions onto a chart: "What did we do right? What went well?" He told the assembled managers that they might find this strange, but he'd like them to consider this question first, then later if they wished they could explore the expected question of what went wrong. In other words, he opted for Solutions Talk before Problem Talk.

Gradually the managers got the idea, and they began to describe what had worked: the crisis had, after all, been dealt with. The customer relations team had responded politely to all the complaints; other managers had come to help as the volume of calls increased; they had swiftly issued a new letter to all the customers, explaining and apologising for the mistake; they had actually lost hardly any customers and were on track for their main commercial goal And so the list went on.

Hans said that they never got to the discussion of what went wrong: by the time they had finished the discussion of what had worked, of what they had done well, they were ready to begin a new list: "What will we do better (the next time)?" All the managers knew what actions they needed to take – not only to ensure that the problem would never arise again, but also to implement and sustain a range of other improvements to their systems that would lead to more efficiency and improved customer service.

(There is a fuller account of this story in the book, Solutions Focus Working, Mark McKergow and Jenny Clarke).

The coach

In this example, we contrast the different directions the conversation might take, depending whether a coach takes a problem or a solution track.

Rhiannon is a finance manager, who has been in her role for eight years. She tells her coach that she would like to be promoted to finance director within her organisation. Then she says, "The trouble is I'm terrified of public speaking, and I know that the finance director has to present at the big management meetings and also to the board. So I'm thinking I won't apply for the job."

The coach picks up on what Rhiannon is seeking, and attempts to overlook the Problem Talk of 'terrified' by rephrasing what he thinks she might want as preparation for the desired new role. He says, "You'd like the job – and to apply for it you'd want to be comfortable to present at senior management meetings and to the board?"

Rhiannon replies, "I'd be able to apply for bigger jobs if I felt comfortable enough to present at senior management meetings. In fact, I have to speak at the next management meeting as my boss is going to be away and he's asked me to present the figures for him."

The coach asks, "You're speaking at this meeting… when?"

Rhiannon says, "On Thursday. It must be some deep-seated irrational fear that I've got, because I know my stuff and I'll tell you what, I can teach, I've been doing that for five years…mind you, that's different as it's to students not peers."

This time the coach is drawn into the problem talk as he says, "This sounds tough. You've got this fear of presenting that is holding you back in your career, and you've been asked to present on Thursday. How long have you had this fear, and where do you think it came from?"

Rhiannon replies, "It started when I was a fifth-form student at school, when I was in a debate. I was shaking, and couldn't think what to say. I'm sure everyone was laughing at me. I guess it's a lack of confidence and a fear of ridicule. Why should I put myself in such an exposed position – it's horrible."

By inviting Rhiannon to explore her fear, it is possible that the coach and Rhiannon will learn more about it, perhaps allowing here to confront it or to challenge or deal with it in some way – or perhaps not. It may be productive, but it is not so likely to take them on the direct route to what is wanted. Let's see how a Solutions Talk conversation might have led in a different direction.

Suppose the coach asks instead about a resource that is potentially useful for achieving what the client wants in relation to the issue of speaking/gaining promotion. Maybe they can side-step the history of the fear and steer the conversation towards the client's resources.

In this alternative scenario, the coach asks, "You've been teaching for that long, how do you do that?"

Rhiannon says, "Well, I say to myself before I start 'Rhiannon, slow down' and then I say to the students that I tend to speak fast and if I do that please can they ask me to slow down."

The coach continues on the trail of resources, "Anywhere else that you teach?" Rhiannon adds, "Yes, I was asked to design a two-day workshop for my peers... I was terrified of doing it, but I slowed my speech down and it was so good that they've asked me back to run it many times now. I just need to remind myself to slow down when I present, don't I?"

The parent

Fourteen-year-old Thomas tells his mother during breakfast, "I want to miss school today. I don't feel very well. There's this science test and I've done hardly any revision, so I don't want to go. I promise I'll do some work at home."

Mother could reply with Problem Talk – and ask about how unwell Thomas feels, or criticise him for the inadequate revision (again!). Or she could take a Solutions tack, noting perhaps, "You've done some revision – what topic did you do?" and find out what he remembers about that. The tack chosen will determine whether or not they have a constructive conversation.

Of course, some people love talking about problems and they can probably find others willing to join them in Problem Talk. If we remember the principle of Solutions – Not Problems – we realise we don't always have to accept that invitation, and that there's the possibility of overlooking a great deal of Problem Talk in favour of discussing solutions – what you and others want, and how you can get it – instead.

Solutions Tools and a strategic approach to conversations

Let's meet the set of six practical tools which you can use either independently or in combination to guide you and your conversational partners through any meeting to make it more constructive.

The Platform is your starting point. It is your topic or subject matter. You have the most useful Platform when you can state what you want (even if this might be only to yourself, and you choose not to be so blunt in the conversation itself). If you have a short statement of what you want, or what you both want ("Let's decide where we'll go on holiday this year") you might explore a **Future Perfect** – a detailed description of what you want. The Future Perfect takes you into the world of Suppose: "Suppose we had the ideal holiday for both of us…. what would it include…?"

Our third tool is **Scaling**. You have already met Scaling in the rating exercise earlier. With Scaling you can create a range from 1 to 10, where 10 is the best it can be for you – your **Future Perfect** – and 1 is the opposite, where nothing of the desired future is happening at all. You can then use various points along the scale as conversational devices. Typically you'd ask "Where are we now on the scale?" or perhaps "How would you know you were one point higher?"

Once you have established a Scaling point, you might ask, "What is it that is getting us that high on this scale?", and the answer of whatever it is that is getting you that high produces a list of Counters. **Counters** – as the term implies - are anything that counts towards getting you to where you want to go.

Counters include resources, skills, know-how, examples of previous success – even willingness of someone to have a go to improve matters. Of course, you can include discussion of Counters in your conversations without having a scale: for example, a teacher might ask a student tackling a tricky question, "What do you already know about that?"

Another useful conversational tool is **The Affirm** – offering an Affirm or a compliment by naming a skill or positive attribute of one of the people involved in the talk. If you are noticing a positive contribution, it may well be worth saying something like, "I'm impressed by your willingness to have another go at talking to this supervisor who's been giving you so much trouble. I guess that takes some courage." A well-placed Affirm can give an amazing lift. To be effective, they need to be experienced by the recipient as sincere and accurate, so always base Affirms on the evidence.

The most constructive conversations result in something being different, which may be people seeing things differently or doing something differently. If it's the type of conversation from which you (and your fellow talkers) want something to be done, then develop a sense for **Small Actions** – the kind of steps that can be taken soon after the conversation finishes.

The ideas for Small Actions may pop up at any time during a constructive conversation. Capture them carefully as you go along. Sometimes it is clear exactly what one or the other person needs to do; sometimes it's better to use part of the conversation to run through your collection of potential small steps and decide which to select.

We shall explore all these Solutions Tools in more detail in the following chapters, and you'll have plenty of practice in using them one at a time and in various combinations in the exercises.

For the moment, let's see how they fit together and relate to our earlier concepts of Solutions Talk and Problem Talk in illustrating a strategic approach to conversations.

A strategic approach to conversations

In taking a strategic overview, we can compare a traditional problem-focused approach with the contrasting solutions-focused approach.

First a problem-focused model.

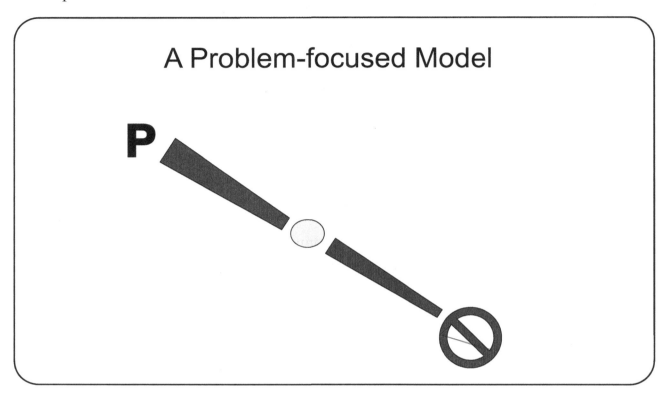

Time is represented along the horizontal axis from past to future.

The dot in the middle stands for the current situation.

The P on the left is a problem – arising in the past. And

represents the dreaded future - what will happen if we keep going in this direction. The red lines connecting these points represent respectively an analysis of how we got from the original problem to where we are now – an exploration of the causes of our current difficulties – and an extrapolation or prediction of what will happen to take us from the current position to the dreaded future.

We call this the Problem axis.

The Solutions Strategy model explores this diagonally contrasting axis, which runs through the same current position.

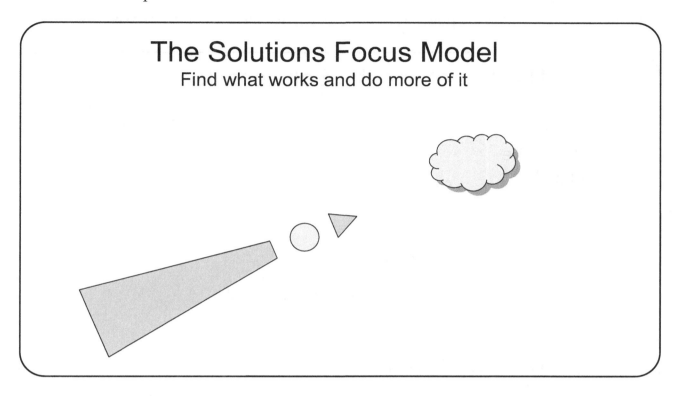

On this axis, the fluffy cloud on the right is the Future Perfect – a preferred state, in which current problems have vanished.

When we look back to the past to discover what it is that has been happening in our organisation, we look at those aspects that are already taking us in the direction we want to go.

This rich body of skills, resources and examples provides the fuel, the encouragement, the motivation and sense of possibility to choose what small step to take next – a step in the direction of the Future Perfect.

Conventionally, we assume that learning about the problem will help with working towards a solution. But here we can see that the problem axis and solution axis are different and independent. Finding out about the problem makes us experts on the problem – which is usually better overlooked.

Once we do more of what we already know works, we can notice its impact and choose to do more of it if it proves useful.

The next diagram overlays the Solutions Tools onto this strategic axis model.

The art of the constructive conversation is to engage people along the solutions axis. Sometimes they will join you there readily and easily; sometimes you can use the tools to help them to switch at some point from the problem axis to the solutions axis.

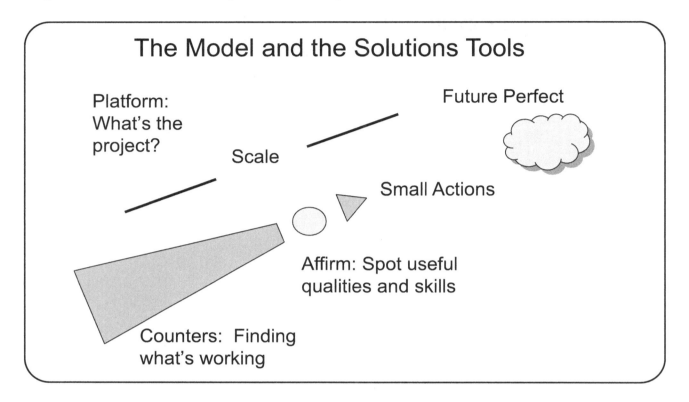

Often the most significant moment in a constructive conversation is shifting people from the problem to solution axis, as show in the diagram below

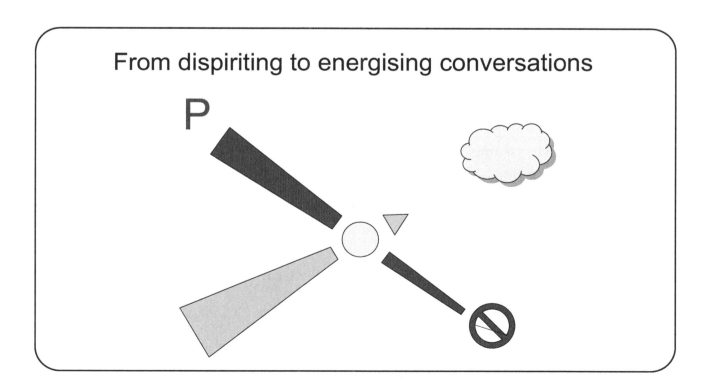

Conversational contexts – putting people at ease

Conversations do not happen in isolation. They take place in a context – and the context makes a difference. The physical space in which we have a conversation makes a difference, as do other contextual factors such as the time of day, the energy levels of the participants, the history of previous conversations, other events occurring at the same time in other places.

Not all of these may be in your control – they rarely are – but often you can have a degree of impact on some of these factors – for example by your choices of where and when to hold a conversation.

If you can choose a congenial place, or arrange the seating to be less confrontational, you can improve the prospects of having a constructive conversation. Perhaps you could have the dialogue while walking – ensuring that you are side-by-side, rather than face-to-face.

If these aspects particularly interest you, you could explore Christopher Alexander's work in 'pattern languages'. Alexander and his colleagues developed a way of describing how certain buildings and spaces have vitality (a cathedral or sports stadium, for example) which others lack (a warehouse with the same volume, perhaps).

He called this the 'quality without a name' and identified detailed patterns that could be applied to describe these things. For example, 'Cosy Nook' describes a space that is somewhat open as well as somewhat sheltered. A bench sitting in an open lawn doesn't show a 'Cosy Nook' pattern, but putting it inside an arc of trees will make it more inviting. Indoors, you can take the same furniture in the same square footage, but make a big difference in how alive the space feels by the way you arrange it. And the quality of the arrangement will affect the conversations you hold there.

We encourage you to experiment with the choice of location and the arrangement of how you are positioned in that space in relation to your conversational partners.

Exercise 1.4
Eavesdropping – Identifying Solutions and Problem Talk

Listen to a conversation between two or more people. Make this a conversation which you are observing, not participating in – perhaps you can safely eavesdrop, or simply ask permission to listen to friends or colleagues. Keep a score – either mentally or on paper – of Solution Talk versus Problem Talk. This means identifying whether each statement you hear is Solution Talk or Problem Talk (or, in probably most utterances, neither).

As you gain skills in attuning yourself to the difference, you improve your ability to decide which sort of talk you will yourself prompt and engage with. It is often possible to minimise or even entirely overlook Problem Talk, in favour of other conversational possibilities, preferably Solutions Talk, which can be continued, developed and amplified.

You can keep tally in the boxes below or create a different format that works for you when capturing this information.

The next exercise is to go beyond noticing and start joining in. The aim is to build your skills at overlooking Problem Talk and amplifying Solutions Talk.

Problem Talk	Solutions Talk	Neutral		Problem Talk	Solutions Talk	Neutral

You can complete these activities by asking people what they have noticed about the conversations – what do they think has gone well for them, and what hasn't?

Finally, how about introducing Solutions Talk, for example at a meeting with colleagues. You might choose a moment to say 'When we did… before, that worked well.' Or 'John is good at this…' Or, 'It seems that what we all want here is…'

Note the response you got and the difference it made.

In a way, Solutions Focus may not be the best title for this approach, because if you ask people whether they are problem-focused or solutions-focused, they tend to tell you that they are of course solutions focused. We're using the term in a more technical sense, which can be summarised in this comparison table:

Problem Focus	Solutions Focus
Talking about problems	Focus on what's wanted
Complaints	Checking resources
Analysing what's wrong	Noticing what's working
Searching for causes of problems	Describing success
Identifying barriers	Identifying useful skills and qualities
Talk of deficits and resistance	Discussing and taking small actions

Looking forward to the next stages of this course

In the next chapter, you will discover great ways to begin a constructive conversation – methods for negotiating a solid Platform on which we can build an inspiring Future Perfect.

Chapter 3 reveals the central importance of discussing what's working, describing the collecting of Counters and several variations of Scaling to enable us to notice, measure and achieve progress. Here we also explore the subtle possibilities of "presuppositional language".

We get to grips with the pragmatics of making things happen in Chapter 4, with the motivational power of the Affirm and the commitment to decisive steps of Small Actions, before putting it all together in Chapter 5 with a range of complete examples from various contexts – including those crucial performance management conversations. By now, you'll be ready to develop your own spins on constructive conversations, aided by our guide to JAM (just-a-minute) Sessions.

In the final chapter we take a more detailed look at how these tools and techniques fit within the intellectual landscape and reflect with you on the progress you'll have made and the progress still to come.

Whether it is with our clients, our colleagues, our bosses; or with our families and friends, we want to get the best out of our conversations. Now you can use these simple, proven tools to hold more effective conversations and get yourself the outstanding results that you want.

Summary of the main points of week 1

○ Constructive conversations are those in which people make progress. The conversation makes a difference.

○ We can have a constructive conversation in any context, and it is worth creating the best conditions you can for such conversations to take place.

○ The art of constructive conversations can be seen as part of a wave of positive approaches to change, and the proposed benefits of holding such conversations are backed by robust research in therapy and positive psychology.

○ Constructive conversations follow the SIMPLE principles of Solutions Focus:

❑ Solutions – not problems

❑ Inbetween – not individual: The action is in the interaction

❑ Make Use of What's There – not what isn't

❑ Possibilities – from past, present and future

❑ Language – Clear not complicated. Use the language of your conversational partners

❑ Every Case Is Different

○ We can identify Problem Talk and Solutions Talk and strategically aim to steer conversation from one axis to the other.

○ We have six Solutions Tools, which you can apply as tactics or steps within your conversations. They are:

❑ Platform building – clarifying a worthwhile topic, involving what people want

❑ Future Perfect – describing in detail what's wanted

❑ Scaling – putting a number against where we are now in relation to what's wanted

❑ Counters – discussing resources, skills, attributes that are getting us towards what we want

❑ The Affirm – identifying and articulating the personal qualities on which we shall be drawing to make progress

❑ Small Actions – describing the possible actions that could take us closer to what we want

References for this week

Jackson PZ & McKergow M: The Solutions Focus – Making Coaching & Change SIMPLE. Nicholas Brealey International 2007. Chapter 4

Levitt S & Dubner S: Freakonomics, Penguin Books, London

Fisher and Ury: Getting to Yes, Penguin Puttnam Inc. London

Alexander C *et al*: A Pattern Language, New York, Oxford University Press

McKergow M & Clarke J: Solutions Focus Working, UK, Solutions Books

Web resources

SOL http://solworld.ning.com/,
UKASFP http://www.ukasfp.co.uk/
EBTA http://www.ebta.nu/

Week 2: Opening the conversation and setting the direction

Take a moment to consider if you ever have conversations where you sense "stuckness". Perhaps you have dialogues where you feel you are making no progress or where you spend time analysing a problem or what's not working. Do you ever experience conversations that leave you feeling drained when the talking is done?

Maybe there are people you talk to who continually blame others for their problems and who refuse to take any personal responsibility. Perhaps you have such conversations with a particular person or in certain situations over and over again.

It doesn't have to be like this. The good news is that you can influence a conversation from the outset, increasing the likelihood that it will be a constructive, useful and energised interaction. You can be Positively Speaking whether it's a talk with one of your team who can't find a way forward, a customer complaining about your service or even a friend who continually moans about their job, their partner or the weather.

What we'll cover this week

This week we'll introduce you to two tools - the Platform and Future Perfect - that will help you start your conversations with solid foundations and an inspiring sense of direction.

We'll introduce each tool in turn, provide some examples and offer you the opportunity to practice using these tools for yourself.

The Platform is the starting point for a constructive conversation, where we shift from talking about the problem (or what is not wanted) to identifying what people do want (the solution), gaining agreement to work on the topic and explore the benefits of doing so.

The Future Perfect is often the next phase of a constructive conversation, and is a rich and detailed description of the desired outcome - how it will be when you or your conversational partner has what they want or when the problem has vanished.

The Platform

Let's start with the Platform.

Meet Elizabeth – a senior manager in a Further Education college. Elizabeth was particularly busy at a time when her college was facing a government inspection. Understandably, colleagues around her were tense. She noticed that she was spending her evenings at home catching up with the work that she hadn't managed to get done during the day.

She realised that too much of her time was taken up with conversations with her staff: anxious about the inspection, they were coming into her office to discuss their worries and concerns. Elizabeth was keen to help them and would stop what she was doing, listen to their problems and then try to fix them. Often the staff member would go away pacified and Elizabeth would have promised to do something to help them. They would then return a day or so later with another issue for her to solve. And so it would go.

Here's a typical conversation that she was having:

Mark:	Elizabeth, do you have a minute? I'd like to talk about the problem I'm having with getting my staff to do their portfolios.
Elizabeth:	Why sure Mark, what's the problem?
Mark:	Well, whatever I do, they don't seem to complete the folders, so I'm behind with my reports.
Elizabeth:	Why do you think they don't complete their folders?
Mark:	Well, maybe they are lazy, or they don't know how important it is – though they should, I've sent them enough memo's about it.
Elizabeth:	OK, how about I drop them a memo and remind them about getting them to you in time?
Mark:	Thanks Elizabeth; that would be great.

Notice how Elizabeth has instantly accepted the invitation into problem talk. By the end of the dialogue, nothing has been resolved and she has now picked up more work to do – with Mark taking no responsibility for fixing the problem.

Elizabeth decided to try something different – she'd been to one of our workshops and liked the idea of platform-building. So the next time one of her staff came into her office, instead of asking for more details about the issue the person brought along, she asked some different questions.

Next time Mark came in it went like this:

Mark: Hi Elizabeth, have you got a minute?

Elizabeth: Sure, I've got 10 minutes. What would be most useful for us to discuss in this time?

Mark: My staff still aren't filling in their portfolios even though you sent the email.

Elizabeth: OK, so given that, what do you want from this conversation?

Mark: Well, I'd like to find a way to get them to do their portfolios.

Elizabeth: OK, so suppose we have a chat about this and come up with some ideas, are you happy to try one or two of them out?

Mark: Yes, I suppose so, something's got to work.

Notice, Elizabeth did something entirely different here – instead of getting drawn into the problem, she built a platform – and by doing so moved Mark from the problem axis to the solutions axis – they are both clear now about what they want and Mark is prepared to do something about it.

Elizabeth told us she continued to start her conversations this way, establishing what people wanted – in one day she said she saved 6 hours, by having more focused, solutions-orientated conversation, rather than broad problem-orientated discussions.

Exercise 2.1
Reflection

Today, pay attention to the conversations you have. Notice whether or not you are encouraging problem talk and where you have made the switch to building a Platform.

What's the difference between the two types of conversation for you?

What are you noticing that is helping you to establish a Platform?

What would you like to pay more attention to in future conversations when starting a conversation?

Let's explore Platform building more closely. Platform building includes:

○ Establishing a starting point

○ Checking that the topic is one worth discussing

○ Ensuring that the person we're talking to is prepared to do something about the topic.

You will save a great deal of time by building a Platform at the beginning of a conversation or meeting.

By building a Platform we are establishing:

○ **Who wants what** – As we saw with Elizabeth, here we can clearly identify what people want from the conversation. This is also an opportunity for you to state what you want from the conversation.

○ **Who is prepared to do something** – Sometimes people want matters to be different yet are not prepared to do anything about it. For example, when somebody wants their boss to do a better job or wants the organisation to change, yet doesn't want to be part of the process of changing it.

Therefore it's important that when we establish the Platform we are clear that somebody is prepared to do something.

○ **What would be the benefits of moving forwards** – Asking about benefits at this stage serves a number of purposes:

    ❑ By exploring the benefits somebody may become more excited or committed to taking action and having a useful and proactive conversation

    ❑ We find out more about what is important to the person, which may be useful information as we progress

    ❑ If there is little or no benefit to spending time on this topic then it's worth finding out early on – allowing us either to stop there, or explore further to find something that the person does want to work on.

We also want the Platform stated in positive terms – beginning with words such as "I want…". This contrasts with the negative grammatical phrasing that people often use when faced with problems or difficulties; typically, "I don't want…"

If somebody told you they didn't want a cup of tea, it's unlikely you would ask them more about the cup of tea that they did not want. Yet in conversations when somebody says (for example), "I don't want my team to perform so badly", the temptation is to ask more about the poor performance of the team – *the 'performing badly' that they do not want.* We are drawn into a conversation about what the person doesn't want – which is unlikely to be useful and will probably centre on problem talk, analysis and little direct action.

It's like somebody examining a compass and saying "We don't want to head North", leaving some 359 other choices of direction to choose – and with little chance of us guessing the best direction. Better to elicit from them that they want to go south-by-south-west.

We know we have established a Platform (and are ready for the conversation to move on) when we are clear that the person or people involved want something to be different and are prepared to do something about it.

Platform building drill

Sometimes people don't know what they want from a conversation or situation; in such cases we can help them by building a Platform together. The platform-building drill below, developed for just this purpose, is adapted from the work of Finnish psychiatrist and solutionist Ben Furman. It goes like this:

Listen to the story – what the person is saying
Here we are listening for clues suggesting what the person may want. For example, if they say, "I don't want to be tired all the time", we might guess that they want more energy. Sometimes we are lucky and they will state directly what they want. "I want more energy when I step into the classroom".

Acceptance
We might say, "That's a tough situation…" Here the idea is to let them know that we have heard them and are willing to acknowledge how it is for them. At the same time, we take care neither to introduce nor get drawn into problem talk.

Building – identifying wants

After listening closely, we will have an initial idea of what the person wants. They may have told us directly or we can make a reasonable guess. At this point, it's useful to say, "So what you want is....?" and for you to state the Platform succinctly. If we get it right first time, that's great and the conversation can continue to its next phase. If not, that's still useful, as the person is likely to build on what you've said or correct your misunderstanding, and together you can get clearer about what they would like to discuss or work on.

Check for benefits

We want to ensure that this is a conversation worth having. Asking about benefits – how making progress on the issue will enhance the life or work of the person – helps to establish and articulate the value in the topic.

Check that the person is prepared to do something

Remember, we know we have a Platform when the people involved want something to be different and are prepared to do something about it, so we check this out here too.

Here's an example from a coaching session:

Coach: What do you want to talk about today?

Listen to the story

Craig: Well, the biggest problem I've got at the moment is Michael. He works for me and I need him to see that there is a problem here - and that he needs to do things differently. I need him to change his behaviour.

Acceptance

Coach: Sounds like a tough situation: so tell me, what would be useful to you from our conversation today?

Building – Identifying wants

Craig: It would help if I could find a way to tell Michael that there's a problem.

Coach: And remind me what is it that you want Michael to be doing…

Craig: I want him to see there's a problem and for him to listen to me.

Coach:　　So what you want is…?

Craig:　　What I want is for him to do what I ask him.

Coach:　　So you'd like some ideas on how to get him to do what you ask?

Craig:　　Yes, that would be useful.

Check for benefits

Coach:　　How is that useful for you?

Craig:　　Well, if I could find ways for him to do what I asked we'd get much better results as a team.

Checking if he's prepared to do something

Coach:　　And if we come up with some ideas, do you think you might be prepared to try them out after this session?

Craig:　　Well yes, I've got to do something about this.

　　　　　Now it's your turn – you'll see the worksheet on page 44. As you listen to somebody, write notes in the appropriate column, then use the platform-building drill.

> Tip:　If somebody states things in the negative – for example, "I don't want to be so busy", or, "I don't want my boss to be hassling me all the time" – ask them what they would like instead.

Exercise 2.2
Platform: From problem to solution

○ Who wants what?

○ Does the person want something to be different and are they (in principle) prepared to do something about it?

○ What would be the benefit in moving forwards?

Case example:

PROBLEMS Note here any problems/negatives or 'don't wants'	WHAT DO THEY WANT Note here what they say they want, or your guess at what they want, given what they have said.
I haven't had a holiday in two years	Wants a holiday
I am very stressed	Wants to be calmer
I'm a terrible listener	Wants to be a better listener

Now use this information to build a platform using the platform building drill:

○ Listen to the story – making notes in the table above

○ Acceptance

○ Building – Identifying wants – with reference to notes in table above

○ Check for benefits

○ Checking if he/she is prepared to do something – even if we don't yet know what that is

You can also establish your own Platform – that is to say, express clearly what it is that you want - at the beginning of a conversation or meeting. For example, as a manager dealing with somebody's habitual lateness, you could say, "I'd like us to discuss and come up with ideas of how you could get to work on time more often – are you happy to have this conversation and try out a few things as a result?"

If you are starting a new project with a colleague, you might say, "We've got 30 minutes for this initial meeting; by the end of it I'd like us to have agreed how we can work well together and have some ideas of how to start this project – is that OK with you?"

Exercise 2.3
Establishing your own Platform

List a few opportunities coming up in the next days or weeks when you think it might be beneficial to establish your own platform.

What you might say in these situations?

Reflection 2.1
Benefits of Platform building

Take a few moments to reflect and note your thoughts about:

What are the benefits – to you and to your conversational partners - of building the Platform in this way at the beginning of a conversation?

How might this contribute to you having more constructive conversations?

Future Perfect

Once we have established a solid enough Platform, our conversations can progress with greater ease and clarity towards the desired result.

The Future Perfect provides a conversational method of establishing a rich and detailed description of what is wanted or of life without the problem.

By establishing a Future Perfect we
- Provide direction for the conversation and the project
- Motivate and influence people – if the future is compelling then they are more likely to be motivated to take action towards it
- Get a detailed description of what people are looking for, therefore making it easier to identify it when it happens – perhaps even enabling us to notice parts of the Future Perfect that are happening already.

Eliciting a Future Perfect enables both parties in the conversation to get a clear idea of what is wanted. And in creating such a full description, you may discover some useful adjustments to the Platform – as you realise that what you thought you wanted turns out to be somewhat different to what you want, now that you have considered the greater detail with all its implications.

Of course, you can hold a Future Perfect conversation with groups, too, as the concept readily lends itself to situations beyond the one-to-one settings that we are focusing on here.

You can use the Future Perfect in a wide range of conversations. For example,
- Checking with a client what they would want as the results of a successful project
- Helping people to become unstuck by asking them about life without their problem
- Developing careers by asking a member of staff how you would know they were doing their job really well.

To get this detailed description of the desired future we ask the person to describe how they would know that things are happening in ways they want.

Coaches often use the Miracle Question, first asked by Insoo Kim Berg when she responded to a client who in exasperation exclaimed, "Maybe only a miracle will help". (DeJong & Berg, 1998). Berg and her colleagues soon discovered the immense utility of asking clients to imagine how life would be in an ideal situation.

Let's take a look at the classic Miracle Question:

Suppose....

You finish your day, go home, go to bed and eventually you fall asleep...

And while you are asleep a miracle happens ...

And the problem that brought you here has vanished

But you're asleep, so you don't know the miracle has happened. When you wake up – what's the first sign you notice that tells you that the miracle has happened?

When the question is answered, you can usually follow up by asking for more details, including:

What do others notice that is different?
What are you doing?
What are others doing?
What else is happening?
How are people responding?
What else? Who else?

You can ask questions about what people are doing, seeing and hearing – building a description of what is going on between people – taking an interactional perspective on this ideal or miracle scenario.

Try this out for yourself with the exercise overleaf:

Exercise 2.4
A miracle for you

Think of a something you want – you really want.

For example:

○ To have a better relationship with somebody

○ For a particular project to go well

○ To be organised and have a balanced life

If you can't immediately think of what you want, choose a current problem and then switch it to what you want as we did above when building a Platform.

With this in mind – read the following question and then write your responses to the questions below:

Suppose….You finish your day, go home, go to bed and eventually you fall asleep

….And while you are asleep a miracle happens

….And this problem has vanished or things are how you want them to be

…..But, you've been asleep so you don't know the miracle has happened. As you wake up – in the middle of the miracle - what's the first sign you notice that tells you things are now as you would like them to be?

What do others notice that is different?

What are you doing?

What are others doing?

What else is happening?

How are people responding?

What is the positive impact of this for you and other people involved?

What else do you notice?

Who else notices what is happening?

Reflection

How was that useful?

What's different for you having explored your Future Perfect?

Other ways to establish a Future Perfect

Now, in some conversations you may feel talk of miracles to be inappropriate. No matter, there are many other ways to ask Future Perfect questions.

Here are the most significant elements required for creating your own Future Perfect questions:

○ **Suppose**

Starting your question with "Suppose" has the feel of a gentle invitation. You are not proposing any commitment; merely proposing an exercise of imagination, a pleasant speculation. This makes it easy for your conversational partner to join you for this visit to 'suppose-land'.

○ **The build-up**

It helps to have some build-up to prepare for the moment when you ask someone to describe life without a problem. You carry them along in your suppositional world with phrases such as "as you leave here today" and "we finish this conversation". They are easy to agree with and create a well-paced transition to give people time to adjust to and answer the question.

○ **Time/space shift** – something that takes the person from where they are to a time and space where things are how they want them to be…..a miracle, or perhaps a holiday, a sudden end to a conversation, some time in the future, waving a magic wand – your choice of how you present the shift in time and space may be a simple or as dramatic as you choose.

○ **Noticing first small signs** – what they and others are noticing.

Here are two examples:

Suppose

Suppose….

Build up

This conversation has been useful for you in some way

Time/ space shift

You leave here and close the door – as you step back into the office, things are now how you want them to be

Small signs

What's the first thing you notice that tells you this is the case?

OR

Suppose

Suppose....

Build up

You have at your disposal a time machine – you know one of those boxes that travels in time

Time/space shift

Suppose you get into this time machine and it takes you to a time and place where this problem has been solved

Noticing

As you open the door to the time machine and step out, what are the first signs you notice that it's taken you to this new time and place?

REMEMBER – we want to hear the person describe in detail what they would be seeing/hearing/doing/noticing, so:

    ○ Focus on tangible, observable change – what's different
    ○ Look for details, simple words, signs that would be visible to the rest of the world
    ○ Stay focused on what's happening, by being present with the 'here and now'

> Tip: If somebody says they are feeling something - for example they may say that they are feeling happy – you can ask them, "What do others notice about you that lets them know you are happy?" This converts the subjective feeling of happiness into a tangible, observable, interactional quality.

Exercise 2.5
Create your own Future Perfect questions

Identify some opportunities in forthcoming conversations when it would be useful for you to explore a Future Perfect with somebody.

Perhaps you have:

○ A performance conversation coming up with one of your staff

○ Work to do with a client on a project

○ To plan a holiday with a friend or partner

○ The opportunity to help somebody think through a problem or issue.

Note here the opportunities you have to explore the Future Perfect:

Now: create some possible Future Perfect eliciting questions below using the framework outlined above.

○ Suppose

○ Build

○ Time/space shift

○ Noticing

Putting it into practice

Have a Future Perfect conversation with somebody – perhaps making use of one of the situations identified in the previous exercise

Reflection 2.2

Having had the conversation, make a note of your reflections by answering the questions below:

What went well for you and for the person you asked about the Future Perfect?

What did you notice was different after the time/space shift?

What are the benefits of these kinds of conversations?

Where could you use this?

NOTE: We have focused on *asking* somebody about their Future Perfect: it's worth noting that we can also *jointly* build one - for example, a manager and a member of staff jointly agreeing what a 'successful' project would look like, or a team building a joint Future Perfect of what 'excellent team work' would mean for them and others.

Conclusion

This week we have explored the Platform and Future Perfect tools, effective approaches for starting and building constructive conversations in various contexts. By establishing a solid Platform you can save time, build relationships and increase the likelihood of having a useful and positive conversation. Then a Future Perfect provides an informative and detailed description of what people are looking for which is motivational and enables them to identify 'success' when it happens.

Next week we'll build on this by working with two more solutions-focused tools, Scaling and Counters.

Summary of the main points of week 2

- ○ We have a Platform when we know that somebody wants something to be different and is prepared to do something about it
- ○ The Platform should be stated with positive grammar
- ○ The Future Perfect is a rich and detailed description of how people want things to be
- ○ Remember to steer conversations to tangible and observable details about change; ask for specifics and signs that would be visible to the rest of the world

References and further reading for this week

Jackson PZ & McKergow M: The Solutions Focus – Making Coaching & Change SIMPLE. Nicholas Brealey International 2007. Chapter 4

De Shazer S & Dolan Y with Berg, Trepper, McCollum & Norman:
More Than Miracles: The State of the Art of Solution-focused Brief Therapy – The Haworth Press Ltd, 2007

De Jong P & Berg I: Interviewing for Solutions. Brooks Cole, 2001.

Week 3: Scaling and Counters: Two new conversational tools

This week we'll explore two more tools, Scaling and Counters, designed for measuring progress and identifying what's working. Together they help us to focus on what's useful and what we might do more of.

The scale is a near-universal tool for measurement, used by doctors to ask patients to measure pain, teachers to rate achievement and on feedback questionnaires to show degrees of satisfaction. It's often used where 10/10 is the desired result and anything below that is not good enough. While perhaps lacking finesse as a motivational method, this introduces many to the basic idea. If you are doing particularly well, you might describe yourself as, "Off the scale!"

Rating and scaling are all around us in life and play a significant part in constructing positive conversations. We can use Scaling to engage individuals in reflection on their own strengths and coping strategies; provide a means of identifying personal goals; indicate steps towards achieving those goals.

Scaling is an accessible and effective tool for constructive conversations because

- ○ It helps the individual and team focus on how they would like things to be
- ○ Asking why people have placed themselves at a certain point helps to elaborate their strengths
- ○ By measuring change it can encourage further change
- ○ If repeated on several occasions it is a way of confirming progress
- ○ It is a means of deciding priorities and next steps

This week we will also explore the Counters tool. A Counter in a constructive conversation is whatever we discuss that is helping us get towards our desired state of affairs. Whether strengths, skills, resources or previous examples of success, a Counter is anything that counts. They show up in many ways including:

- ○ Where the solution (what is wanted) happens already
- ○ Where parts of the solution happen already
- ○ Something resembling what is wanted happens already

○ Resources, skills and qualities that may be useful

○ Grounds for optimism that things may be about to improve

○ Evidence for being up to a certain point on a scale

○ Others' knowledge, skills and experiences

Scaling

Here's an example of Scaling at work:

Jane is a supervisor for the wines and spirits department of a large supermarket and is struggling to get all her tasks done – she is feeling overwhelmed. She goes to her manager for help.

Jane: I'm really struggling – I need to find a way to be more organised and manage my time better.

Manager: OK, so on a scale of 1-10 where 10 is you are as organised as you want to be and are managing your time very well and 1 is that you are totally disorganised all the time – where would you say you are on the scale?

Jane: I'd say I'm at a 3.

Manager: A 3 – so tell me what makes it a 3 rather than a 1?

Jane: Well I'm not totally disorganised; I got my children to school on time, the staff rotas are done and I'm pretty sure we put all the right pricing on the products this morning.

Manager: That's encouraging; tell me what else makes it a 3?

Jane: I guess I can get organised; when I've got time I write detailed lists and am pretty good at sticking to them.

By asking Jane a scaling question and then asking her how she had got that high, the manager and Jane start to find what's working – ie Counters. A function of Scaling is to develop confidence in what has already been accomplished. This in turn leads to hope of accomplishing more in the future.

Notice how it is Jane - the person with the issue - who chooses the number on the scale. If it is Jane who identifies she's at 3, she now owns this and cannot resist working with this number. If her manager had given Jane the number, she might have disagreed, leading to a discussion or debate about the number rather than one about progress and moving forward.

The conversation now continues, with the manager steering Jane towards possibilities of progress.

Manager: So, you have some experience of being organised and awareness of how to go about achieving this. I've also noticed how accurate you are when you do the rotas – this is very impressive given how busy you are.

Jane: Thank you - I've just been so overwhelmed recently, I forgot how to get organised.

Manager: You placed yourself at a 3 on the scale. Tell me, what would be the first thing you would notice if you were at 4 on the scale?

Jane: If I was at a 4, my desk would be tidy – I would have an orderly in-box and a clear space to work in.

Manager: So given this, what's a small action you can take in the next days or weeks that will move you up the scale?

Jane: That's easy, I'm going to spend the last half hour of today sorting through my paperwork and clearing my desk.

Notice how Jane's manager complimented her and asked her about how to get to 4, rather than straight to 10 – prompting small actions rather than large heroic ones. Had the manager asked Jane straight away how she could get to 4 or perhaps 10, it's unlikely she would be able to answer this – if she knew what to do she would probably be doing it already.

The scenario opposite illuminates a difference between how scales are used in a problem-focused and a solutions-focused way. Taking a solutions focus includes using the scale to explore progress made (1 to n) rather than focusing on a gap, such as the entire distance still to be covered (n to 10).

Had the manager asked Jane how come she was only at a 3 or why she wasn't at a 10, they would have had a different conversation – most likely centred around problems and deficits, blame and justification.

The diagram below shows the contrast between using scales in a problem-focused and a solutions-focused way:

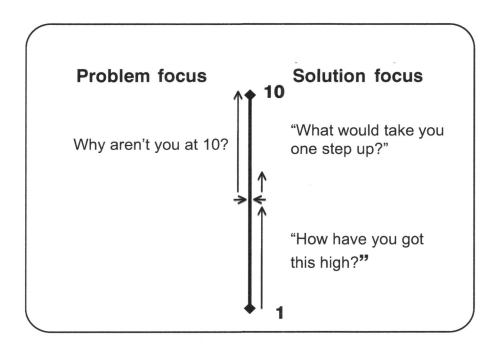

We can also use scaling to explore differences or 'shades of grey' as solutions-focused trainer and author Peter Szabo describes them. Jane might be at 3 today, yet it's entirely possible that she may have been higher on other days or perhaps in other situations.

Manager: You're at 3 on the scale: when you think back over the past months what's the range of where you have been on the scale?

Jane: Well, it varies quite a bit depending on what's going on, I'd say it ranges between a 2 and a 6.

Manager: So what were you doing differently at that higher point of 6?

Jane: It's a 6 when my desk is clear – so I guess it's when I've managed to get my filing done.

Manager: And what do you suppose others, such as your team might have noticed was different about you when you were at 6 on the scale?

Jane: They would have noticed that my desk was tidy and that I could find whatever they asked for quickly – I knew where everything was.

Manager: How did you manage that?

Note the possible temptation here to ask about the 2. Instead the manager chooses to ask about the differences with attention directed to what's happening at 6. This positions the manager to ask about Counters – whatever Jane knows or has done that will help her reach her goal of being more organised. Jane's manager also asks what others would notice when she was at 6 on the scale, bringing in the interactional element, the 'I' of SIMPLE.

We can also use the scale to ask about the best it has been. The manager could ask Jane what's the highest she's ever been on the scale of being organised and then explore that occasion - what she was doing, what colleagues might have been noticing about her at this time.

The manager also has the opportunity to explore 10 – another way to establish a Future Perfect.

As you can see, Scaling proves a useful and versatile tool for making progress within constructive conversations.

So far we have explored using scales where we are asking a person to rate their own performance. We can also use scales when eliciting feedback from others. In the scenario below, Richard, a recruitment consultant, is having a conversation with one of his clients about a recent project he's been working on:

Richard: It's good to have this opportunity to check-in and see how the project is going.

Client: Yes, there are a few things I wanted to speak to you about regarding how you've been going about filling this post.

Richard: OK, let's take a scale from 1-10 where 10 is you're very happy with the service we've provided and we are meeting all your requirements and 1 is that you are very disappointed with our service and your requirements have not been met at all. Where would you say things are between 1 and 10 right now?

Client: That's an interesting question; I'd say it's a 6 right now.

Richard: A 6: so tell me what are you pleased with and what's working that makes it a 6.

Client: Well, you've got a great understanding of our needs which was reflected in the detailed person specification you sent out, and you work fast – we were very impressed that you got so many CVs to us in such a short time.

Richard: Thank you, we do like to be efficient. Tell me, what would make it a 7 on the scale?

Client: A 7 would be that you had filtered the CVs a bit more before sending them to us – instead of sending over the 15 you did, we'd rather you got that down to 5 which would save us time.

Richard: That's fine, we can do that….

Here Richard has applied Scaling to create a constructive conversation about his performance and what he can do to make progress.

When Richard heard "6", he might have asked how come it was a 6 not a 10 – then he and his client could have had a detailed discussion about all the aspects that were disappointing and not working. This would put Richard on the defensive, perhaps less motivated to remedy matters, and would have focused the client's attention on every unsatisfactory element of the service – unlikely to suit Richard's desire to retain this client. Instead, by discussing how come it was a 6 and what was working, the client had time to reflect on what he was pleased with, providing some clues and positive feedback for Richard and a reminder to the client of what he liked about working with him.

In this instance, the client measured Richards's performance. The same tool can measure much else. In conversation you can scale for:

○ Performance: On a scale of 1-10 where 10 is the desired performance and 1 is the opposite, where are you on the scale currently?
○ Confidence of progress: On a scale of 1 -10 where 10 is you are absolutely confident you will make progress and 1 is that you have no confidence in any progress being made, where are you on this scale?
○ Commitment to action: On a scale of 1-10 where 10 is you are as committed as possible to taking this action and 1 is you have no commitment to take this action at all, where are you now?

When using Scaling in your conversations here are a few guidelines:

○ Invite the person with the issue/the client to say where they are on the scale – rather than telling them where you think they are.

○ Accept the number they choose for themselves on the scale – the number in itself is not immediately significant: what matters is what it helps you to elicit about their situation.

○ When the person gives you a number – resist the temptation to ask how they might make progress and ask instead about how they got that high. When people are stuck they don't know what to do next, so there's often little point in asking them straight taway what will move them up the scale. By exploring first what's got them as high as they are on the scale, you will uncover clues as to how they might make progress.

○ Scaling is a means of exploring individuals' perceptions rather than fixed reality – so be flexible and open to exploring the whole of the scale.

○ State what 1 and 10 are, with 10 being the desired outcome/the Future Perfect or what the person wants and 1 being the opposite.

○ When establishing 1, make it likely the person will place themselves on the scale above 1. In the example above, 1 for Jane is being totally disorganised all the time. It is unlikely that she will say that this is the case, so Jane will probably place herself higher than 1. This provides the opportunity to explore how she got that high.

○ If somebody does say 1 or 0 – don't panic! Remember we can explore 'shades of grey': you might ask them how come it's not minus 5, or you might ask them to tell you when it has been a bit higher. A low number also invites you to ask questions about how they are coping. You use the number to draw attention to what they are doing well, what resources they have and anything else that might be useful in terms of making progress.

○ Be aware that not everybody needs or wants to get to 10. We were recently talking to a classical guitarist, for example, who wanted to start playing the guitar again having not played for a while. She had previously performed at concerts and played to an exceptionally high standard. She described 10 in great detail, including her performing on stage with people applauding her. Then she commented that she wouldn't want to be at 10, as while it was wonderful to be on stage, the amount of practice and effort it took to do this was far more than she was prepared to commit at this time. So we asked her what would be good enough and she said she would be happy with 7.

○ When asking for small steps invite the person to tell you how they can get one step higher rather than how they can get straight to 10. Here the emphasis is on movement towards what's wanted rather than being at 10. Of course if they can get straight to 10, then that's great.

○ Before moving up the scale, it's sometimes useful to ask people how they can keep the number they have – so the manager might have asked Jane how she proposed to maintain her 3; then they could focus on making progress.

○ Make it interactional where possible. As you explore the scale, invite the person to speculate about what their colleagues/clients/friends/boss might notice about them when they are at 'n' on the scale. What skills and attributes would others say the person possessed that enabled them to get to that point on the scale?

Exercise 3.1
Playing the Scales

Think about some conversations you would like to have – perhaps they are some of those you wrote about last week or maybe other conversations you are likely to have in the following days or weeks.

Given what you now know about Scaling, what opportunities do you have to use scales in your conversations? List these below.

Pick 2 or 3 of these opportunities and write down what you would say 1 and 10 are for these Scales:

Counters

We mentioned Counters earlier, noting that people have useful knowledge, skills and experience that they can apply when they want to make progress. We can also find useful Counters or know-how from other people. The search for Counters is an important phase of many constructive conversations.

We elicit Counters by turning our talk to the following categories, aiming to identify them, make them open and explicit, and - of course - put them to work:

- ❍ When the solution (what's wanted) happens already
- ❍ When parts of the solution happen already
- ❍ Something resembling what is wanted happens already
- ❍ Resources, skills and qualities that may be useful
- ❍ Grounds for optimism that things may be about to improve
- ❍ On a scale from 1 – 10, where are you now? How come it's that high?
- ❍ Others' knowledge, skills and experience

Let's explore each of these in more detail:

- ❍ **When the solution (what is wanted) happens already**
  This is when the desired outcome already happens periodically in the person's life or has happened at least once - preferably not too long ago.

During a coaching conversation with us, Carl was complaining about John, one of his team members, who didn't respond to requests for information and was generally unhelpful. Carl said he was at his wits' end and was considering disciplinary action against John. Once we had established the kind of conversation Carl would like to be having with John, we asked him, "When was the last time you had a conversation like this with John?"

Carl considered the question for a while, then answered, "About two weeks ago. I asked him for his help on a project and he was very accommodating." We asked him what was different that time. Carl replied that often he called John on the phone or asked him to come to his office (which was at the other end of the building), yet on this occasion he had visited John in his office – and he strongly suspected this was what had made the difference.

From then on, when possible he went to John's office. To Carl's delight John started responding to his requests and became much more helpful. What Carl wanted had already happened, the questions just helped him to re-arrange what he knew and then put it to use.

○ **When parts of the solution happen already**

Sometimes parts of what's wanted are happening. Let's meet Alice, who felt that her work life was totally disorganised: she was missing appointments, her office was a mess and she couldn't find important documents. She wanted her life to be more organised. After a short discussion, we discovered that there was one drawer of her filing cabinet that was tidier than the others, the one that held all her personal documents. By exploring how she managed to get this one part of her life organised, we uncovered Counters that helped her organise other areas of her life too.

○ **Something resembling what is wanted happens already**

Sometimes what is wanted isn't happening exactly, but we can find something sufficiently like it to construct a possibility of progress.

Debbie had recently completed a coaching course and was keen to start her business, but was struggling with the idea of selling her services. She had previously been a manager in a large organisation and had never had to directly sell her work.

Our conversation took place shortly before Christmas, when Debbie mentioned that at this time of the year she made and sold jewellery at local markets. Seeing an opportunity to uncover some Counters, we asked her how she sold her jewellery. Debbie explained this process in detail and then realised that she did in fact have experience of selling and marketing her work. She said she had started selling her jewellery by sending flyers out to friends and letting them see her work.

Inspired, she did similar things to grow her coaching practice, and within three months she had a healthy list of clients.

○ **Resources, skills and qualities that may be useful**

During our conversations we can often identify skills, qualities and resources applied in one situation that may be usefully transferred to another.

Janet, the mother of three young children, had the ability to can stay calm when one of her children had tantrums. Having identified this quality she was able to stay calm when colleagues were getting agitated and disruptive at work.

○ **Grounds for optimism that things may be about to improve**

In conversations about especially tough situations, it may not be so easy to discover the Counters. Our search may be appearing fruitless as our conversational partner fails to come up with examples of when they have succeeded at the task to hand or even at similar tasks. This is when it's worth articulating any signs of optimism that matters may be about to improve. Perhaps you would comment that the person who you are having difficulty working with turned up to your office to have a conversation with you. You might simply ask, "Well, this is very difficult: what's giving you hope here?"

When things seem tough for somebody we can ask them how they are coping, then identifying and highlighting their resources which can build resilience and the ability to handle the situation.

○ **Scaling on a scale from 1 – 10, where are you now? How come it's that high?**

As discussed above, Scaling is an excellent and versatile way to uncover Counters.

○ **Others' knowledge, skills and experience**

Sometimes the people directly involved in your conversation have useful experience, skills and knowledge, and you can gather enough Counters to make progress from these alone. Sometimes it's useful to hold a wider search for Counters, asking yourselves who else you know or have heard of that has expertise on these matters.

Counters in action

To ensure that the Counters you collect are relevant, keep in mind what the people in the conversation want – staying on a solutions track, rather than getting tempted into finding examples of the problem and its associated phenomena.

Meet Robert, a high-ranking executive who wanted some help.

Robert: I really need to be healthier. I had cancer a few years ago and fortunately recovered. Yet I still eat unhealthy food, I don't exercise much, I'm overweight and I work very long hours. I know if I keep going like this it's likely to kill me, but I just don't seem to be doing anything about it.

Coach: So you want a healthy lifestyle and to live longer?

Robert: Yes, it seems so obvious, yet I'm doing nothing about it. You'd have thought I'd have learnt by now.

Note the temptation here might be to explore the problem. The coach might be tempted to ask Robert why he wasn't doing anything; perhaps we could explore how devastating it would be for his family were anything to happen to him. This might be interesting in some way, yet it is most likely to lead to unhelpful analysis and rather depressing problem talk – neither of which are likely to motivate Robert to take action.

Instead the coach looks for Counters:

Coach: Tell me Robert, was there a time recently when you were a little bit healthier?

Robert: Yes, when I first started this job, I was very careful about what I ate; I avoided the corporate lunches.

Coach: How did you do that?

Robert: It was simple really; I just planned ahead a little. I would bring lunch in with me and if I didn't, instead of eating big work lunches I'd head out to the local deli and get a healthier sandwich. I just don't have the time for that now.

Coach: Tell me more about times you have been healthier.

Robert: I used to go out in the evenings for walks after work; that was refreshing and my son would come with me. It was a good time for us to catch up. My son's at university now so I don't go for walks.

Coach: So you used to plan ahead and go for walks after work?

Robert: Yes, things were definitely better then.

The conversation continued with Robert outlining the benefits of having a healthier lifestyle and looking for more Counters.

We spoke to Robert a month later.

Coach: Robert, of all the things you've done since we last met, what's better?

Notice the coach starts the session straight away by asking for Counters.

Robert: Well, I thought about our discussion last time and remembered how I used to plan my food. I thought that I didn't have time to do this, but I do have a PA who can organise things for me. I asked for her help and she's been great – she rings ahead at corporate lunches and orders healthy food: she makes sure there's sandwiches and salads available when I'm in the office. It's made a big difference.

Coach: That sounds really useful – what else is better?

Robert: This idea of going for walks. I realised that I don't like walking on my own, so now my wife walks with me when she can. We get to go out maybe once or twice a week and I've been thinking of joining a rambling club as I like company when I walk. There's still room for improvement here, but it's a great start. For the first time I'm feeling motivated to do something about this.

By uncovering Counters, Robert developed clues about what could work for him, and these appear to have motivated him to take action.

Counters questions

Here are some questions you can use in your conversations when exploring Counters:

What are you doing well that is getting you to 'n' on the scale?

What makes it 'n' as opposed to 1?

When does what you want happen already? Even a little bit?

When do parts of what is wanted happen already?

When do things like what you want happen already?

What do you suppose you did to make that happen? How did you do that?

What personal qualities will help you achieve the outcome?

What personal qualities would your boss/colleagues/clients/friends say you have that would help you achieve this outcome?

When have you been in a similar situation and succeeded…what did you do? What was different?

Where else in the organisation does this happen?

Who can help you with this?

What do you/we want to keep – what's working already?

What else do you know that will be useful for us when working on this project/topic etc?

What has worked before?

What's working already?

That sounds like a tough situation – how are you coping?

Who else may have useful know-how in the team or beyond?

What's better since we last spoke?

Counters from others – a wider search

We would recommend that your search for Counters starts with the person whose issue you are exploring – what do they know that will usefully help them make progress? It's important to find Counters that fit well, those that will work for the people who want them to work. Like a pair of shoes, the best fit comes directly from the people who'll be wearing them.

Once we have explored these Counters, we can extend the search, looking for Counters from a variety of sources – the people you're working with, other groups within the organisation, other people in your social circle and beyond.

You may find yourself having a conversation where you have some Counters to contribute. This is fine – making sure that what you give is offered as a gift rather than as a direct instruction to do something.

One way to share your know-how and offer Counters is to tell a story. Humans have regaled each other with stories to pass on knowledge, wisdom and experience since time immemorial – our oral tradition predates written culture.

For constructive conversations, we can tell stories from many different perspectives.

Caroline is a freelance facilitator; she has had a successful year and is wondering if she should take the next step of expanding her business by hiring some associates or staff. She is also looking for some advice about how to do this.

We might choose to use stories to share ideas with Caroline. There are a number of perspectives from which we can tell our story – let's explore this below.

We might choose to tell her '**My story**' – a story from your own experience. This can build your credibility and show that you have had similar experiences..

> *"I went through this myself, Caroline, when I got a very large contract with an organisation. I sent a request out to a trainers network list, asking for people with the relevant experience to contact me. I got loads of replies and found three people who were ideally suited to the work. They worked with me as associates and together we have successfully and enjoyably delivered a number of projects…"*

When telling 'My story', take care not to wrench the conversation into becoming all about you.

Another option is '**His or Her story**' - a story about someone else, a third party, perhaps known to both of you. This can prove exceptionally useful, as by talking about somebody else you indicate no particular attachment to the story, leaving the person free to decide to what extent it is useful. This can also be used to share one of your own experiences without having to talk about yourself.

> *"Caroline, let me tell you about my colleague Bob, who was in a similar situation to yours. He looked into the legal and financial side of employing people and decided that it looked like a lot of paperwork which he didn't enjoy. So instead, he increased his day rate. This enabled him to earn more from the work he was doing so he didn't need to expand his business."*

Perhaps this is an area in which you have expertise, so you have an '**Expert story**' to tell. This can be useful when the person wants specific advice. Use with caution, as if you position yourself as an expert, the person may feel obliged to follow your advice. Also, taking the role of expert may lead to you doing the work and appearing responsible for the person's actions. It's most productive to take the 'Expert' stance when you suspect they will draw confidence from the credibility you have in respect of the topic.

> *"Caroline, as you know, I have set up a number of successful businesses. Each time, I went through a systematic process of analysing the market. I developed an associate network and hired a number of support people so that I wasn't bogged down in paperwork. I've written a paper 'How to go from one to many', which I'd be happy to pass onto you."*

We might offer the person a **'Metaphor or Legend'** – a story which is tangential to our topic, perhaps appearing at first glance unrelated, but which may suggest a new way forward for the customer. This has the benefit of lateral thinking, inviting the listener to interpret it in their own way, taking whatever strikes them as useful.

"Caroline, let me tell you a story: Once there was a man who sat on the side of a river, fishing. He was very good and caught many fish. One day a businessman was passing and noticed how successful the fisherman was. He told the fisherman that as he was so good at catching fish, he could catch many fish, sell them and would soon be able to afford a boat. Once he had the boat he could catch more fish, then extend that boat to a fleet and catch more fish, thus making lots of money. The businessman said to the fisherman, "Just imagine what you could do with your days then." The fisherman replied, "Yes, then I could fish all day."

Tips for telling stories
- Make them relevant so that they are about the subject and tailored towards what the listener needs.
- They should be empowering – stories of success. Avoid stories of failure and despair.
- Fill them with resources and ideas.
- Make them fraught with possibility and choice.

Exercise 3.2
Sharing Stories

Think of some advice you would like to share with somebody.

What is it? Write it here.

Now write it as a story from the different perspectives:

My Story

His/Her Story

Expert Story

Legend or Metaphor

If you get the opportunity – try these stories out with the person and ask them which was most useful. Which perspective did they prefer?

The language of Counters

"To question is to wield a powerful linguistic blade. It is necessary to ensure the blade is used to reveal strength and beauty rather than to carve away these same qualities"
(An international model of questions and therapeutic interventions by Dan McGee)

"There are questions which illuminate, and there are those that destroy: ask the first kind."
(Isaak Isador Rabi – Nobel physicist)

You may have noticed certain qualities of the questions and statements used for exploring Counters and for having constructive, solutions-focused conversations. They are often pre-suppositional, leading people towards solutions talk and to identifying what's useful, uncovering their resources and positive attributes. Let take a moment to explore this further.

Consider the client we met earlier in the chapter who is living an unhealthy lifestyle. We have a choice. We can explore the cause of the problem, in all probability the deficiencies of the person, by asking, "So why are you living such an unhealthy lifestyle even though you know it might kill you?" or "What do you think might be wrong with you?" or "What other ways will your unhealthy lifestyle impact negatively on your life?".

Or we can take a solutions focus to reveal strengths and resources by asking questions such as, "When have you been healthier?" and "What do you know that's useful about living a healthy life?" and "Suppose you started living a healthier life, what would be happening?"

Notice the presuppositions in each set of questions. The first set presupposes fear, bad experiences and future failure. The second set presupposes resources, skills and a positive future. For conversations to be constructive, it's our task to choose the words for our questions and statements wisely – phrasing them so that they presuppose people have resources, skills and attributes that will help them achieve what they want.

Our questions then encourage people to explore what's possible and to identify and work with their strengths and those of others. Questions phrased in this way are also likely to encourage solutions talk rather than take us on problem-focused excursions.

Exercise 3.3
What is pre-supposed?

What do each of these questions pre-suppose?

Question	What it pre-supposes
How did you know how to do that?	The person has some knowledge, experience or skill that enabled them to do this
When have you been further up the scale?	
Of all the things you've done since we last met, what's better?	
What else?	
What will be the first sign that this conversation has been useful for you?	
When was the last time you made a good decision?	
What did your boss see in you that led her to choose you for this project?	
What did you contribute to the outcome?	
Given all your experience of this kind of thing, what do you know about what would be useful in this situation?	
Which of your many skills did you use in this situation?	

Note below what else you are noticing about the way these questions are formatted:

Summary of the main points of week 3

○ Scaling and Counters are tools for measuring progress and identifying what's working, what's useful and what we might do more of.

○ When using scales, accept the number the person chooses for themselves on the scale – the number itself is not important, what matters is what it helps you to elicit about their situation.

○ Start your search for Counters with the person whose issue you are exploring – what do they know that will usefully help them make progress? You can then extend the search, looking for Counters from a variety of sources.

○ Build your questions using positive, resourceful and pre-suppositional language.

References and further reading for this week

Jackson PZ & McKergow M: The Solutions Focus – Making Coaching & Change SIMPLE. Nicholas Brealey International 2007. Chapters 5 & 7.

McGee D: An Interactional Model of Questions as Therapeutic Interventions. Journal of Marital and Family Therapy, October 2005, Vol 31, No4, 371 - 384

Szabo P : Scaling for coaches - 10 minutes for performance and learning. http://www.solutionsurfers.com/start.php?id=resources/furthermaterial

Szabo P & Berg I: Brief Coaching for Lasting Solutions. W.W Norton & Company 2005.

Mid-course Assessment

Congratulations! You have arrived at the half-way point of this program. In the spirit of employing multiple avenues for learning, we would like to offer you the opportunity to reflect on and apply what you have learnt so far by putting the solutions-focused tools to work.

You are going to use multiple scales to assess your progress and plan the next small steps you will take to continue your learning about constructive conversations.

Turn to page 81 of this book where you will see five scales ranging from 1-10.

○ The top scale represents your overall competence to have constructive conversations. 10 means that you are completely competent in conducting and participating in such conversations and are confident that you can apply all the tools consistently and effectively in all the contexts you wish to. 1 indicates that you have heard the phrase 'constructive conversations' but have yet to apply any of the available tools in your work or at home.

The following 4 scales represent sub-competencies for having constructive conversations. These are:

○ Listening for resources – being able to hear what's useful, identifying Counters
○ Solutions Talk – asking questions and making statements that encourage Solutions Talk (not Problem Talk)
○ Responding in the moment – the ability to adapt and respond to what is being said
○ A competency of your choice – insert here a competency you think is important for you to have and develop when having constructive conversations

For these scales 10 is the best you would wish to be at this competency and 1 is that you have heard of the competency, but do not use it to affect your conversations in any way.

On each scale put a cross for where you would place yourself now.
There are now a series of questions for you to answer in relation to each scale.

Finding resources

We'll start with the top scale - your overall competency with regard to solutions-focused constructive conversations. Noticing where you have placed yourself on the scale, answer the following questions:

○ What are you pleased with that you have done to get as high as 'n' on the scale?
○ What's helping you perform at that level?
○ What do you suppose you did to make that happen?
○ How did you (know how to) do that?
○ What else has got you that far?

Shades of grey

Now, we are gong to explore 'shades of grey'. Choose one of the sub-scales – whichever you want to work on first - and mark on it the range within which you operate for this competency. For example with 'listening for resources' you may have a range between 3 and 6. Once you have marked the numbers on the scale, write your answers to the following questions:

○ What was different between the two points?
○ What were you doing differently at the higher point?
○ What would others have noticed about you that was different at the higher point?
○ What else?

The best it's been

Picking one of the sub-scales yet to be explored, take a moment to think about the highest you have been on that scale; perhaps it was a memorable conversation or a specific moment within a conversation. Now mark on the scale where that was and answer the questions below:

○ What was it about this moment that made it so good?
○ What were you doing that contributed to it being so high on the scale?
○ What would others have noticed about you at that moment?
○ What else is useful for you to remember and note about what you were doing?

Exploring 10

Choose a different sub-scale. You are now going to explore 10 by answering the questions overleaf:

○ Suppose you are at 10 for this competency..........how do you know?

○ What are the first signs that tell you are at 10?

○ What do your colleagues, team, boss notice that tell them you are at 10?

○ What else are you noticing or is happening when you are at 10?

One more scale

With your final sub-scale, make a note of any counters, knowledge, skills or resources that are relevant to having got you this far on the scale.

Affirm

As you look back on the notes you have written about the progress you have made – what are you impressed with about your skill and ability to have constructive conversations? Note this below:

Small actions

Pick the two scales that seem most important and relevant to you. For each of these competencies identify and write below small actions that you'd like to take and that could raise you one point further up the scale. Choose actions that you can take within the next seven days.

Small actions for scale _____

Small actions for scale _____

Multiple Scaling worksheet

Your overall competency at having solutions-focused constructive conversations

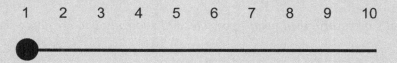

Listening for resources

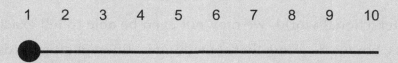

Solutions Talk and Problem Talk

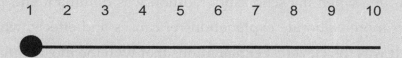

Responding in the moment

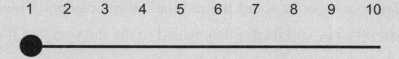

A competency of your choice

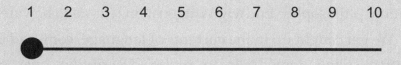

Week 4: Making things happen

"Start by doing what's necessary, then what's possible, and suddenly you are doing the impossible."

St Francis of Assisi

A constructive conversation is usually one with a purpose. At least one of the people engaged in dialogue wants something to be different. The conversation itself changes things, or change happens as a result of the conversation.

In a complex, interactional world, we may not even be able to tell exactly when or where the change occurs, but we do know that something is different afterwards. In this sense, the conversation is pragmatic.

Pragmatism is a philosophical tradition. We can trace it back, for example, to William of Occam, a British philosopher in the 14th century, whose legacy is Occam's Razor. Occam was writing at a time when the scholastic tradition was dominant and philosophers were constructing ever more elaborate explanations of causes and effects, why things were the way they were. It was the cleverest explanations that won the most applause and did most to build the philosopher's reputation. Occam was unimpressed and his Razor proposes that we seek the simplest explanation that can account for the facts.

The Razor has proved useful, for example, in the development of physics. Both Newton and Kepler offered plausible theories about the motions of the planets. Newton's was simpler, needing fewer assumptions, and its predictions led to the discovery of the planet Neptune.

Over the centuries since then, psychologists such as Alex and Janet Bavelas have demonstrated that humans have a tendency to be swayed by complexity, to be too ready to accept complex explanations where simple ones are perfectly adequate.

In the same tradition, philosopher Ludwig Wittgenstein tells us to beware of the bewitching power of words. We get caught up in the currents of language, confused by vocabulary and arguments. Wittgenstein's remedy is to prefer description over explanation. For constructive conversations, our preference when dealing with complexity is to avoid the fruitless quest for explanation – the analysis of cause and effect – and instead stick to description – stating what can be observed, using concrete, detailed specifics. This helps us avoid speculation, fault-finding and unprovable probes into supposed phenomena – such as what we imagine is going on in other people's heads. It helps to keep us in an interactional world, with a focus on what makes a useful difference.

Our conversations are kept purposeful and have a bias towards action rather than understanding (although people will often feel understood when they experience the good listening that is an important part of a constructive conversation).

This week we'll explore two practical aspects of conversations that make useful differences, The Affirm and the Small Action. We'll develop the theme of responsiveness, drawing on the pragmatic theatrical tradition of improvisation, and learn a detective-style activity that helps us deal far more constructively with people who tend to complain.

The Affirm

"I can live for two months on a good compliment." Mark Twain

Before you resolve a conversation by somebody deciding what action they will take, it is often a good idea to affirm the things that are going well, and to articulate the resources that will help to fuel that action.

Questions to ask about the conversation so far include:

What have we identified that's going well?

What are you/we contributing to making that happen?

What attributes, skills and resources have we been demonstrating?

What is impressing us?

What can we admire?

What is it about you that gives us hope that there will be progress here?

The answers to these questions will typically result in a list of qualities, resources, skills and attributes. The Affirm is when one person expresses these positive attributes or qualities – usually in a short, pithy compliment.

It seems to me from our conversation that you really care about the welfare of that customer.

I'm guessing you have the dedication to get your homework in on time.

It sounds like it's important to you that this is dealt with fairly.

You strike me as an optimistic person.

Not many people would have had your courage to confront that director.

The role of The Affirm is to articulate the positive quality – to put it on the table, so that it is plainly visible, enabling the recipient to pick it up, appreciate it and use it to make progress with the task at hand.

People perform better when they are appreciated. What can you find to appreciate in the suggestion that your colleague is making? What attributes of theirs do you value? What skills and qualities do you suspect they have that will be particularly useful for the immediate challenge? Mention these during the conversation and notice the impact they make. Remember, conversations are interactional – what can you do to help them to help you?

Because the Affirm is one of the subtlest and most under-used tools in the Solutions Focus kitbag, we are going to give you plenty of tips about how to use it effectively, and opportunities to practice it widely and often. We were once asked by a manager of a British company what would happen if Affirms were over-used in an organisation. We replied, "We don't know – it's never been tried."

To be most effective The Affirm should be
○ Well-directed – highlighting a quality that will be useful for the project
○ Experienced by the recipient as sincere
○ Based on evidence, or at least a strong hunch: if it is a hunch, say so
○ Offered as a possibility - if someone resists the affirm, don't insist. (They've heard you anyway and may be demurring politely, while still taking in the implications of the compliment).

It may take skilled detective work first to identify the resource and then to name it briefly and at an appropriate moment.

Not all Affirms are direct statements. You might wrap an Affirm inside a pre- suppositional question. For example, after hearing about a string of efforts - perceived as failures by the person trying to get something done – you might ask, "How can we ensure that all your hard work doesn't go to waste?"

Exercise 4.1
What I like about your idea – finding value in each other's suggestions

You can practice this exercise with a willing colleague as a pair. Or you can adapt it so that only you need know what is going on.

It's described here for a pair who each want to practice the affirming skill.

Make a note of this pattern of language on paper or somewhere visible to you both.

Write:
A chooses a topic which B is prepared to accept.

A:	'Let's …. [makes suggestion]'
B:	'Yes, what I like about that idea is…. [finds value in the suggestion]…
	'And…. [makes new suggestion on same title topic]…
A:	'Yes, what I like about that idea is…. [finds value in the suggestion]…
	'And…. [makes new suggestion on same title topic]…
Etc	

Now one of you is A, the other B, and you have a conversation using this format. For example, A proposes the topic of 'designing a new table', which B accepts. Using the pattern above,

A says:	'Let's design a chair made of wood'
B replies:	'Yes, what I like about that idea is that wood is a traditional material. And let's have a chair that is bigger than standard chairs.'
A:	'Yes, what I like about that idea is large people will find it more comfortable. And let's carve animal shapes into the arm-rests.'
B:	'Yes, what I like about that idea is it will give people sitting in it something to look at. And let's price it at £40….'

And so A and B continue to alternate until the design is complete or the conversation runs out of energy. Other good practice topics might include a car-park of the future; tidying my office; planning a holiday you will take together (you don't actually have to go on it).

Discuss what you found interesting and useful about the practice conversations. When we introduce this activity to a group, we speculate on what would happen in an organisation if managers used the expression 'What I like about your idea' once a day. With thanks to Sue Walden from whom we learned this activity.

If you can find value in what someone says – even if you don't happen to agree with their suggestion – you can keep your conversations on a constructive track. It's an adroit means of avoiding the sorts of unnecessary arguments that can easily flare up when someone feels they have been put down or not listened to.

The next exercise, developed by Rayya Ghul, is a technique for finding resources when someone is moaning or complaining. You use an Affirm to shift somebody from complaining to the beginnings of a constructive conversation.

It also serves as an advanced practice for developing listening and affirming skills. It's advanced because while it is relatively easy to develop an Affirm when somebody is talking about what's gone well, it can take greater skill to do the same when someone is moaning. Here, the idea is to turn a complaint into a constructive conversation.

Exercise 4.2
Moan, moan, moan

Next time you are in a conversation when someone complains about something, your task is to listen to the person's complaint with your constructive ears. This means not getting involved in the topic, even if you have an opinion about it. Instead listen for the person's skills, attributes and talents and then feed them back to the person when they've finished.

It's essentially detective work – spotting and naming skills, offering your evidence to support the Affirm when necessary.

You might say, for example, "I'm impressed with your ability to keep calm when talking about something that annoys you so much".

You can either practice this with a partner, when you both know the nature of the activity, or you can be a secret affirmer, trying the technique during a real, natural conversation.

If you are practicing with a partner, take it in turns, with one of you complaining about something for up to one minute, then allowing the other to affirm. When you have finished, ask yourself:

How was that for you?
What was that like for the complainant?
How might that be useful in your conversations?
What other ways can we respond to somebody complaining, and how useful are they?

When somebody complains we have many choices, and often we are tempted to join in, to tell the moaner to go away, to compete with bigger moans of our own, tell them they don't really a problem, or (a particular favourite in organisations) attempt to fix it for them.

With all of these responses we are either joining them in the issue (problem talk), thus making it bigger, or giving the impression of not listening to them which will also increase the likelihood that the complaint will not go away.

Expressing gratitude

As Robert Biswas-Diener tells us in his Flexible Learning study guide, Invitation to Positive Psychology (p50), expressing gratitude is perhaps the best-known positive psychology intervention.

By expressing thanks and appreciation, we create a powerful affect for both the recipient and the giver, articulating contributions and our positive feelings about those contributions.

Improvisation skills for constructive conversations

"It is not the strongest of the species that survive, nor the most intelligent, but the one most responsive to change."

Charles Darwin

As we have discussed, interactions are at the heart of constructive conversations. In Solutions Focus we have a saying: "The action is in the interaction". And because each interaction is unique – in context or content - it takes an element of spontaneity to give it value.

We hold conversations in a practical paradoxical place where you need both structure and freedom; planning and instant response; a general awareness and the agility to work with whatever emerges. This is the territory of the improviser.

Whether you are a manager, a teacher, a coach or a parent, you gain a huge advantage when you can comfortably respond in the moment as your conversations develop.

You get closer to your strategic goals by developing fluency in your tactics.

Of course, in most conversations we are improvising constantly. If we understand improvisation as the exercise of freedom within a structure, your general plan or your coaching model (OSKAR, GROW or a selection of SF tools) provides a structure, and it is within this that you make choice after choice.

As you develop your improvisation skills, you get better at making more appropriate responses. This takes you deep into your:

❍ Listening skills
❍ Ability to be present
❍ Responsiveness
❍ Creativity

so that you and your conversational partners can enrich every session. In the next section, we see what each of these might mean.

The skills you need

From the traditions of drama and performance, we already know that important skills of improvisation include:

○ **Listening skills** – the performer's first duty is to listen to what is happening in the scene, so as to join (or continue) precisely that scene. If they have not been attentive and aware, they are going to upset the audience by appearing to lurch into a different reality. This tends to look either selfish, careless or both.

○ **Ability to be present** – the state of being ready in the here and now; avoiding distractions of past or future and awareness wandering elsewhere.

○ **Responsiveness** – the ability to respond in the moment to the signals around us and to our own relevant processes.

○ **Creativity** – the ability to come up with something new and useful at just the moment that it is needed.

How these connect to conversational skills

You'll need all the above skills if you are to progress beyond formulaic conversations. It is fine to have a structure – the advanced coach, for example, uses freedom within that structure, and it is improvisational skills that equip the coach to use the structures to best advantage. We can usefully think of this as the coach being a highly-skilled performer in the client-coach conversation.

A positive, affirming attitude turns out to be crucial both for successful improvisation and successful conversations. The idea is to say 'Yes,' whenever possible in response to what your partner offers. In dramatic improvisation, saying 'Yes' to a partner's offer during a scene is the most important way to keep that scene going. For a coach, it is part of accepting a client's story. For the manager it's staying on the same side as your reports, and for the parent it's connecting more closely with the child.

This way of working also reinforces the interactional principle of staying on the surface - rather than questioning what you are hearing because you think you have a better idea of what is 'really' going on for them. In improvisation and constructive conversations, you work with what you get, not looking to impose pre-thought theories or to search for hidden meanings. Meanings emerge in the course of the conversation.

An improvisational performer becomes expert at leading and at following, and at knowing when each is appropriate. Likewise, you will be in a 'dance of conversation' with your partners.

Theatrical improvisers are trained to make their partners look good. Similarly, your success in conversations is inextricably linked to the success of your partner as you develop ideas together. SF pioneer Insoo Kim Berg spoke of 'meeting clients in their resources' and would achieve this by asking them about their successes and appreciating whatever skills and qualities she identified in them. When they looked and felt good, her work looked good.

This improvisational attitude introduces a more playful quality into your conversations. You develop your sense of possibility, of flexibility, an optimism that things might be different and can work out well.

Being playful enables you to be both purposeful yet less attached to the outcome. While you can be optimistic, you also realise that we do not control the future. "What happens, happens". We work with what emerges, aiming to nudge it in useful directions.

Each conversation takes us into the unknown. The improvisational conversationalist expects the unexpected and is willing to work with whatever arises, with a focus on careful listening: this builds a relationship in which you are likely ultimately to get more of what you want.

Dialogue – by definition – is an activity of turn-taking. It helps to keep your turns short, which means being comfortable with silence, waiting when necessary for your partner to take their turn. If they need time to think, that's fine – these may be the most valuable moments of the entire process.

Affirms to prompt and fuel action

In constructive conversations, The Affirm is often closely connected to action, putting your partner into a resourceful state, feeling ready to take action – prompted by the reminder of their relevant skill, and empowered by appreciation.

One purpose of an Affirm is to create positive emotion in the recipient and research suggests that positive emotion improves performance. In one study, medical doctors receiving small gifts from researcher Alice Isen and colleagues made better and more careful diagnoses than doctors who didn't receive gifts.

Barbara Frederickson proposes that positive emotions make us more curious and more experimental – useful qualities for the feeling of safety and the need for creativity for more constructive conversations. In one study, for instance, Frederickson showed that people induced into a good mood were more likely to want to try new things and to engage in a much wider range of activities than their emotionally-neutral counterparts. If your conversational partners are feeling more positive, perhaps they'll also be in a more receptive mood for the ideas you wish to propose.

Swedish consultant Bjorn Johannson demonstrates the power of The Affirm spoken by a manager in an industrial setting. Introducing solution-focused practices into a Kraft factory, Bjorn's team heard of a worker who was responsible for a date-stamping machine. As the packages came off the production line, he was supposed to spot when this rather old machine started to malfunction and began stamping the wrong dates.

He was very poor at this job, and tended not to notice the mis-stamping until many packages had gone through – costing the company a great deal of money. The managers thought they had tried everything with him – gentle reminders, posters stressing the importance of watching the machine carefully, motivational talks, small punishments, threats of further discipline, even considering replacing the machine which would have been very expensive or sacking the worker, which would have caused difficulties with the union.

When the manager learned about The Affirm he decided it would be a good tactic to use. However long the machine ran incorrectly, he would let it run until the worker eventually spotted and corrected it. At that point the manager would quietly affirm the worker for stopping the machine and thank him sincerely for saving the company money with his action. Unused to this treatment, the worker soon took pride in his ability to spot faults in the machine, and got quicker and quicker at stepping in and putting things right.

"The first key element of e-culture is that strategising has to become less like following a script, where you know everything about what you're going to do before you do it. Instead, it should be more like improvisational theatre, where you have a theme. Then you develop the details of the strategy by interacting with your audience – the broad range of people who can have an impact on your business, be they customers or critics.

You learn very quickly from their reactions, you make fast modifications and you move onto the next version of your product. You don't do long tests and rollouts any more."
Rosabeth Moss Kanter, article in Organisations and People, February 2002

Actions – small steps

Successful change frequently hinges on small actions that people take. The action gets us unstuck and helps us to move effectively in a world that changes in complex, that is why small actions should be a big topic in your constructive conversations. Who is going to do what?

Small actions have several advantages over big actions. They are both easier to propose and easier to take. They require less confidence and less energy. Therefore they are more likely to be taken.

And it may be that a small action is all that is needed to get a situation unstuck. The new circumstances that then arise may be more conducive to further easy action.

A small step has less chance of severely disturbing other people who may be involved. If they are suddenly faced with huge changes, they may start to resist, whereas a small alteration may be less noticeable and less challenging as the change begins.

Small actions also have more of an experimental feel. If they work, we can do more of them. If not, we can have another go, trying something else.

The kinds of actions to discuss and subsequently take fall into two basic categories:

1. Doing more of what works
   - ❍ The most likely to succeed
   - ❍ The easiest
   - ❍ A random choice of what might work
   - ❍ Noticing what works
   - ❍ Acting as if the Future Perfect had arrived.

2. Stopping doing what doesn't work and doing something different
   Usually something from the first category will suffice, but if it does not, then doing something different in relation to the topic under discussion may be the best action to take.

Questions to ask include:

If you were to take a small action in relation to what we've been talking about, what would it be?

What actions might we take that stand a good chance of getting us closer to what we want here

What are the next small steps for each of us to take?

You are at 'n' on the scale now; what would it take to get you one point higher?

What else needs to happen?

What's the smallest step we could take?

British coach Jane Lewis, who was coaching children in a primary school in the UK, tried to include this question towards the end of each of her brief conversations with a child: "If you were to make yourself a promise as a result of our conversation today, what would it be?"

Small actions should also be:

○ Specific

○ Be able to be taken in the next day or week

○ Tangible – doing or noticing rather than thinking about something.

It is desirable that the person with the issue decides the small action, engendering responsibility for the next steps.

As discussed, the smaller the action the better. So, what do you do if somebody tells you their next step and you think it's a rather large action, or if you're not convinced it's a well-chosen action?

The temptation here is to challenge them to come up with a smaller action or to question their ability to choose appropriate steps – this can have the impact of making the person wrong, leading to disagreement. Some suggestions for questions should you wish to check the suitability of the small action include:

What's a small step you can take towards this action?

How will this action help you achieve what you are aiming for?

On a scale of 1-10 where 10 is very confident and 1 is not confident at all, how confident are you you'll take this action?

On a scale of 1-10, how confident are you that this is a well-chosen action that will lead to progress?

What are the benefits to you and others of you taking this step?

Exercise 4.3
Why Small Actions?

List the possible benefits of a conversation including talk of small actions

Why small actions rather than big actions?

Why small actions rather than no action talk at all?

Select a forthcoming action-oriented conversation and pay particular attention to the size of actions chosen. Is there greater prospect of progress occurring if the actions selected are made even smaller?

Short Story – a conversational and coaching tool

Sometimes you can take a conversation beyond asking for a single small action, creating a richer, more compelling account of what you would like to happen next. The Short Story is a brief account - by one or more of the people involved in the conversation - about how things are going to be next time they face the issue that they have been discussing.

Let's see how this conversational tool might work. Within a company, two or more people might have a conversation about changes they would like to have happen. As you know, our view is that change is happening all the time. And the conversation itself is frequently a part of that change (possibly a very important part). As Steve de Shazer's Freudian book title says, 'Words were originally magic', and conversation is one arena in which magic is performed.

De Shazer was a prime developer of Solution Focused Brief Therapy (SFBT), and it is common for therapists in this tradition to give their clients a task. The task is something for the client to do – generally before the next therapy session. This sounds rather like the classic action point familiar to people who work in organisations. The organisation typically has a plan, and to fulfil each part of the plan, each member of the organisation has a list of tasks or action points.

Yet there is a different degree of expectation in those two different contexts about whether or not the task is going to get fulfilled. After all, the relationship between a therapist and client has a different quality of authority from that between a coach and a performer or a manager and a member of staff. The question of who is telling whom what to do alters the status of a task, a suggestion or an order.

It also alters the consequences that might be expected from the task-giving. In organisations, if a manager gives a direct report a task to do, everyone normally expects that the task will be done and that the consequences of the action will plainly contribute to the goal being achieved. In therapy, this may or may not be the understanding. Perhaps the task-giving is designed purely to provide more feedback and information about the situation; it may have little to do with any direct achievement of the goals.

One option for constructive conversations is to be less concerned about tasks, and especially less concerned than in a traditional model about whether or not the task is done. This is less shocking than it might at first seem, once we appreciate that task-giving from this perspective is entirely a matter of suggesting possibilities and not directly to do with achieving organisational goals. It is free from the complicating questions that tend to arise in an organisation about responsibility, contracts and promises.

With the precursors to SFBT, the given task was often paradoxical – that is, contrary to what was eventually supposed to be the outcome. The aim was more to break a stuck pattern. With the transition to SFBT itself, there was less focus on stopping of what was wrong (with the consequent paradoxical tasks). Instead the first focus was on doing more of what was already working. The tasks became more about noticing what was working.

The Small Action

Tasks designed purely to break stuck patterns and the noticing task are the direct ancestors of our Small Action – one of the Solutions Tools described in the book *The Solutions Focus* and further developed for this study guide.

Let's look at these ideas in more detail in coaching conversations. In a typical coaching session, the Small Action is usually chosen by the client. It is supposed to be genuinely small, easy to do, happening soon, and within their agency. It may (or may not) be an action point, and many clients' who are used to action points within an organisation and not particularly interested in these subtle distinctions simply choose the sort of action point with which they are already familiar. And that is fine.

The Small Action is a tool to be wielded with skill and care. We are interested in the other person choosing their small step well. The ideal step arises from the possibilities generated during the conversation, and may be checked for their commitment to taking it and for their belief that it will make a useful difference.

In the interactional world, when the action is executed it creates ripple effects or changes in the dynamics, and progress is made – with a well-chosen small action leading to progress towards a Future Perfect.

In sports coaching, the next step for an athlete is typically the practice of a particular skill, such as a tennis stroke or sprint start, or toning a set of muscles in a body-building regime. Often this is based on the expert knowledge of a coach, who has in mind a fitness regime or new skill development. These steps are more like organisational action points than therapeutic tasks.

Exercise 4.4
Small Actions

Make a list of small actions you would like to take today and tomorrow.

The tension

The apparent similarity between organisational action points and Small Actions can lead to a tension in the choice of action. The coach has in mind something small and the customer in the organisation is thinking big. He is more used to a heroic kind of action that gets closer to getting a goal achieved. The organisational action point is a step along the way in a well-thought-out plan, and it directly helps to reach the goal. It is not there purely to create movement, with the particulars of the action almost irrelevant. The action is designed to create benefit for the organisation, not something entirely personal to the client.

Avoiding this tension, some solution-focused therapists do not aim to include talk of action for their clients to take. Their conversations consist of building a clearer vision of the preferred future and an unearthing of resources. Then they simply see what happens. This appears to put less pressure on clients, who by definition are already under stress and strain. There is no need to force them into action. They'll do things or they won't, in any case. If there is no agreed action, then there is no consequent feeling of vulnerability from failing to carry out the action. And no consequent blame of self or of the therapist or of the method, if the action happens to be missed or leads to a worse situation.

It's a danger in a coaching relationship if either the coach or the client gets too hung up on an Action. The question can arise of 'Why didn't you do it?' or 'Was it done well enough?' It can lead to defensiveness or even argument, which are generally unhelpful routes. Preferably, the Small Action is the best idea that occurred at a certain moment in a coaching conversation. It may or may not help, and if someone has a better idea about what to do twenty minutes or a day or two later, then there's at least as much reason to go with the new idea.

Enter the Short Story

In some conversations, the Short Story can usefully be deployed before or after the Small Action or it can replace it.

The Short Story follows a spoken or unspoken recap by one of the speakers of the most memorable, meaningful, significant or useful parts of the conversation so far. It tells how things are going to be when they next tackle the issue that is under discussion.

It is based on the Platform and imbued with all the magic of the conversation, including the pertinent aspects of the Future Perfect, the finest of the Know-how and Counters, and the considered and sifted collection of possible actions gathered along the way.

We've noticed that a Short Story often happens spontaneously during constructive conversations. For example, we heard that one senior executive we were coaching wanted to improve her presentation skills. She had been told her presentations were dull, and during the session she described what a really terrific presentation by her would be like (Future Perfect) and told me about the best presentations she had given in the past (Counters), and the coach offered her some tips (Know-how) and Affirms.

Then we invited her to describe what would happen at her next presentation, and she explained in detail the warm-up process she would use immediately before the meeting, how she would have her notes organised, the way she would breathe during the opening moments of speaking, how she would maintain eye contact with the audience, and so on, through to the reaction she expected at the end – namely one or two colleagues coming up to tell her it had been better than they had anticipated.

Another client, a chief executive, wanted coaching on dealing more effectively with the media. He began his Short Story by saying, 'I know exactly what I'm going to get interviewed about this week – and here's how I'm going to handle it," before describing how he would confidently use the techniques we had been exploring during the coaching conversation.

Rehearsal and visualisation

The Short Story in these and other cases seems to work as a visualisation or mental rehearsal, as the speaker assimilates all the most relevant and useful information from the earlier parts of the conversation.

It is an additional tool, leaving open the possibility of a Small Action, such as an initial action point, or a noticing task, in the more traditional ways described earlier. An action point might remain an excellent idea, for example, if someone expects to go away with one and believes it will be useful.

As you and your conversational colleagues talk through the Short Story there is a palpable sense of these events happening. People sound more confident, motivated, plausible and in control of all the details.

Exercise 4.5
Small Actions

During your next constructive conversation, finish the talk with a short story – encourage your conversational partner to join you in detailing what will happen next time you are dealing with whatever issue has brought you into this conversation.

Make the story as precise, detailed and positive as you can.

Summary of the main points of week 4

○ Occam's Razor reminds us to remain pragmatic, value simplicity and beware the lure of making things more complicated than necessary.

○ Use The Affirm to articulate skills and resources that are likely to contribute to progress.

○ Find value in what your conversational partners are saying – it will help you and them to get more of what you want.

○ Encourage spontaneity and improvisation skills:

   ❏ To build our ability to handle whatever comes up, riding over the bumps inevitable in any interactional situation.

   ❏ To sharpen our receptivity - so we can learn new skills and be open to new experience.

○ Use the improvisation idea of 'Yes… And' to affirm and build; 'Yes' to affirm and 'And' to build.

○ Talk about small actions – to keep conversations leading to action. Small steps are more likely to be taken than large steps; it takes only a small action to get matters unstuck; success from small steps builds confidence for taking the next steps.

○ Create a Short Story to describe in precise detail what will happen next time you tackle the issue under discussion.

References and further reading for this week

Biswas-Diener R: Invitation to Positive Psychology, week 2 and week 3, Capp Press, UK, 2008

de Shazer S: Words Were Originally Magic, WH Norton, 1994

Moss Kanter R: article in Organisations and People, February 2002

Week 5: Putting it all together

Welcome to week 5 of the course, in which you will extend your understanding and application of the tools and principles that we have explored and applied in previous weeks. We'll:

○ Share with you an outline and strategies for follow-up conversations, introducing ideas and options that will assist you to continue having constructive conversations.

○ Explore the idea of 'putting positive difference to work', applying the solutions tools and principles specifically to the art of having constructive performance conversations.

○ Review the solutions-focused tools before putting them to work by creating your own JAM sessions – short and concise lists of questions related to a specific topic that you can use with yourself and your colleagues.

Follow-up conversations

Ideally we move things on in a single conversation, yet often it takes more than one conversation to construct or sustain something worthwhile. In our first conversation we will be establishing our platform, exploring counters, possibly scaling, affirming and agreeing small actions.

We may decide that one conversation is enough and has delivered the desired outcome. Even then, a second conversation may have benefits:

○ People may not have noticed positive progress – a follow-on session often provides opportunities for us to explore what has worked and what's better.

○ It enables us to compliment people on their successes and resources, building the relationship and sustaining momentum.

○ We may re-establish the platform. As we know, we live in a complex adaptive world where circumstances change rapidly. We may need to adjust the platform as what we want changes in response to what has happened.

○ It offers an opportunity to find counters – if something is working it's useful to identify and note it so that it can be used for this topic and for future conversations and projects.

○ We can assess progress and agree further small actions.

Trevor, a director of a small recruitment firm, was having difficulties working with his business partner. During the first conversation he had complained that his partner treated him like an employee rather than a partner. We had a constructive solutions-focused conversation with Trevor and he went away to take small actions relating to how he would interact with his business partner.

Trevor was happy with the conversation and confident that he now knew what to do - and he arranged a follow-up conversation just in case he needed it. We met a couple of weeks later and he started the conversation by telling us that he'd been so busy dealing with a new client that he hadn't managed to take any of the actions he'd wanted and that he was disappointed with himself.

We chose to overlook his disappointment and asked him instead what had gone well in the past weeks. Trevor thought about this for a while, then listed a number of good experiences he had had. These included a productive staff meeting, the hiring of a credible PR person and further development of the business plan. We then asked him what he had noticed about what was better about his relationship with his business partner. Trevor immediately listed a series of improvements in this relationship. He had noticed that when hiring the PR person his business partner had left it to him to make the final decision. In the staff meeting both partners had contributed equally, which was a significant improvement. The list went on.

When we asked what he thought he might be doing to have made these things so much better, Trevor answered with a number of actions he had been taking, surprised that he hadn't noticed them. He left the conversation pleased with himself and equipped with a number of tools to go with his greater awareness about what he was already doing and could be doing to improve his situation. Had we not had this follow-up conversation, Trevor may never have noticed the progress he had made, nor realised that he was already taking useful actions towards what he wanted.

Starting the follow-up conversation

When starting a follow-up conversation, it's tempting to ask straight away about the small actions that were agreed. We suggest avoiding this as a first line of inquiry. Should you ask somebody about their actions and they have not taken them, it may lead to defensiveness, justification and problem talk about what has not been done. This is rarely constructive and may undermine all the good work and progress achieved earlier.

It is also possible that:
- ○ Something else may have been done that was more useful
- ○ The platform may have changed, so the step was no longer relevant
- ○ They had good reason not to take it.

We want to start our follow-up conversations by looking for counters, finding out what's worked and what's better. Keep the conversation on the Solutions axis rather than encourage problem talk. Once we are on track, our options include all the tools – such as affirming resources, scaling, and of course establishing the platform for this conversation.

We often start second conversations with the question or theme 'What's better'.
You'll notice the pre-supposition here that something is better. In the box below you'll see a suggested structure for a follow-up conversation.

Suggested follow-up session format

1. Review

Explore what's better from different perspectives.

Whilst you may not ask all these questions, don't be afraid of repetition. Ask 'What else is better?' as long as it continues to be productive.

What's better?

Since we last met, what's better?

What else is better since we last met?

Of all the things you've been doing since we last met, what's better?

What would your friends/family/colleagues say, if I asked them, "What's better?"

2. Counter finding

Continue the counter search by asking for specifics about what has been done and achieved. Ask for details of what went well and what was their contribution. Use the opportunity to affirm skills and achievements as they are revealed. Again notice the pre-suppositions in the questions.

I guess some of the things you've mentioned were not easy to manage.

How did you manage to do them?

Tell me in more detail.

What skills did you use?

What else was helpful?

Of all the things you've accomplished since we last spoke, which are you most satisfied with/proud of?

What is it that's particularly pleasing about that one?

3. Scaling

Use scaling to measure progress and uncover more counters.

Where would you say things are right now on a scale of 1 to 10?

What's the main thing keeping it that high?

What's the difference between this point and where you were last time?

Where might other significant people put you on the scale?

Which of your skills/strengths/abilities here is most apparent to them, would you say?

How could you make use of the skills/resources we are discussing here in other areas?

4. Small actions

Having reviewed progress so far, check if there are any actions that now appear to be the right steps to take.

How can you keep things going at least as well as they are now?

What small steps could you take to lift you even a little further up the scale?

Who or what will help in maintaining the progress you have made so far?

Who or what will help you make further progress up the scale?

On a scale of 1 to 10, how confident are you that you can maintain these improvements?

5. Platform

Check if the conversation needs to continue and- if it does - renegotiate the platform.

Have things improved enough for you now?

Is there something else we can usefully deal with right now?

What's better – a practical example

Our aim of discussing 'What's better' is to engage our partners in a resource-based conversation. When we run workshops we are often asked, "What do you do when the person says that nothing is better?"

This presents a conundrum as, on the one-hand, the temptation is to follow the person and ask how and why things have gone wrong; on the other, that is unlikely on the face of it to be a conversation about resources. An exploration of what's not working seems less likely to result in the client feeling resourceful enough to find a way forward – and the latter is our more important objective.

Here is an example of a coach putting the solutions tools to work.

Mary is the Human Resources manager at a bank. She is finding it difficult to fit in since taking the job three months earlier.   In particular, she has problems at management meetings, where she feels colleagues ignore her opinions and suggestions.

Coach: Mary, what's better or gone well since we last met?

Mary: Nothing, it's still as bad as it was last time we spoke,

What do you, as the coach, say next?

There are various possible approaches to this reply:

Inviting Problem Talk

One of the most tempting (and perhaps natural) is to explore what's not working – the problem-focused approach.

Coach: Mary, what's better or gone well since we last met?

Mary: Nothing, it's still as bad as it was last time we spoke.

Coach: That sounds tough for you, tell me more.

Mary: Well, I walked into the meeting and as usual they're all talking about golf and the dinner parties their wives arranged at the weekend and being the only woman I am totally ignored.

Coach: Last time you mentioned a small action you could take; how did that go?

Mary: Terrible; I said I was going to get my items moved up the meeting agenda before the meeting, as they often get to my things last when there's very little time. I went to the Managing Director's PA, who just sat there, painting her nails, telling me that the agenda was set and there was no way that I could change it. She was really horrible and I felt like the whole job was hopeless.

By exploring what's not working, the coach allows Mary to drift into problem talk, starting to describe the issue as 'hopeless'.

Let's see what might happen if we take a more constructive tack.

Silence

One solutions-focused option is to remain silent until your question is answered:

Coach: Mary, what's better or gone well since we last met?

Mary: Nothing, it's still as bad as it was last time we spoke.

Coach: (says nothing and waits)

Mary: (after some time) ……well, there was a moment in the last management meeting where Tony seemed to engage with what I was saying and supported my suggestion for monthly staff supervision meetings, but that was it.

This offers a useful opening, a time of slight improvement, allowing the coach to explore this Counter

Coach: That sounds promising; tell me, how did you do that?

Scaling for 'not so bad'

Coach: Mary, what's better or gone well since we last met?

Mary: Nothing, it's still as bad as it was last time we spoke.

Coach: That sounds tough; tell me on a scale of 1-10 - where 10 is how you would like meetings to be and 1 is that you may as well not be there - where are you now?

Mary: About a 2.

As Mary proposes a 2, the coach can assume some elements of what Mary wants are already in place.

Coach: Tell me, what is it you're doing that makes it a 2 rather than 0?

Mary: They do talk to me, you know; ask me how things are going … and they hired me onto the board because they recognised that they needed a strategic HR person. Also sometimes they do respond to what I'm saying.

Coach: Really, OK, when did that happen?

Mary: …well, there was a moment in the last management meeting where Tony seemed to engage…

The coach's gentle probing for instances that run counter to the notion of 'nothing better' turn up a recent example, and the conversation can explore what Mary and/or Tony were doing to have their moment of engagement. That is to say, the conversation is about the conditions under which Mary gets what she wants – colleagues taking notice of her suggestions during management meetings.

Looking for Counters - resources or evidence of success somewhere else that may be useful here

Coach: Mary, what's better or gone well since we last met?

Mary: Nothing, it's still as bad as it was last time we spoke.

Coach: Sounds like you've had a tough couple of weeks.

Mary: Yes, it's been difficult to get things done.

Coach: You have managed to get things done?

Mary: Yes, some.

Coach: Tell me more about that?

Mary: Well, I did get the Finance Director to agree to participate in the induction process. He actually offered run a mini-workshop, and not just do the usual 10-minute overview. This was the final piece of the induction process for this year.

Coach:	That sounds productive; tell me how did you manage to do that?

Mary:	I went to see him, explained the overall idea for this year's induction and asked him what he thought new starters really needed to know about the finance department.

Coach:	And how did he respond to this?

Mary:	That's the interesting thing. Normally in meetings he's very dismissive of me, yet this time he seemed really interested and keen to help.

Coach:	Mmm, how did you do that?

Mary:	Now I come to think about it, I was well prepared with lots of documentation to support why we were expanding the induction and I asked him what he'd like to see rather than telling him how it was going to be.

Mary starts to appreciate that there is more than one way for her to get her work done, and may also decide to adapt her approach to the management meetings.

Discover what was useful from the last session

Coach:	Mary, what's better or gone well since we last met?

Mary:	Nothing, it's still as bad as it was last time we spoke.

Coach:	So, tell me what do you remember from our conversation last time that was useful?

Mary:	I remember we talked about different approaches I've taken in the past that worked for me.

Coach:	Such as?

Mary:	Being prepared for the meetings, bringing statistics with me.

Coach:	What else?

Mary:	Having meetings with people before the meetings and getting support for my ideas before the meeting takes place.

Now Mary is talking about what's worked for her in the past, the coach is on track for a more resource-based conversation this time – perhaps by asking which colleagues appear the best prospects for responding to such an approach, or perhaps by changing tack and discussing Mary's other skills.

Asking coping questions

If we cannot gently unearth something better, the coach can look for what's stopping it from getting worse.

Coach: Mary, what's better or gone well since we last met?

Mary: Nothing, it's still as bad as it was last time we spoke.

Coach: That's tough: How have you coped?

Normalise

Coach: Mary, what's better or gone well since we last met?

Mary: Nothing, it's still as bad as it was last time we spoke.

Coach: Well, it's not unusual to feel like this when you're the only woman in a management team. I have other clients who've had this problem and over time they've found ways to become part of the team and get themselves listened to.

Mary: Really, that's encouraging; I thought it was just me.

Affirm

Let's assume we heard from Mary that she had tried to speak to the PA, who she describes as 'a scary person', so we can affirm the action that she took.

Coach: Mary, I'm impressed that you actually attempted to speak to the MD's PA - she sounds like quite a scary character.

Mary: Yes, that's true, she is rather scary and it's the first time I've had the courage to ask her to change something. I hadn't thought of that.

Slightly alter the question

This can be a useful starting point if you suspect for some reason that your conversational partner is more than likely to take a plunge into Problem Talk.

Coach: Mary, of all the things you've been doing since we last spoke, what's better?

Mary: Of all the things.......well, I've managed to get the induction process off the ground, and my team are doing some good work there.

Coach: That sounds promising, how did you do that?

Mary: The final thing I needed to go ahead was for the Finance Director to agree to get involved, and I managed to do that.

By asking 'Of all the things you've been doing', the coach has broadened the range Mary can choose from, leading to a more resourceful conversation.

Any of these solutions-focused options stands a chance of shifting Mary from the problem axis to the solutions axis, putting the coach into position to ask Mary what she wants from this conversation.

It's apparent that there are many routes into a constructive conversation, even when the situation appears to be one of little hope.

People saying that 'Nothing is better' does happen, though surprisingly not very often. We have discovered that people work hard to answer questions and will try to find something that's better even in very difficult circumstances. The skill is in the timing and application of the questions. Insoo Kim Berg, one of the originators of the solutions-focused approach, said, "If you want to go fast, go slow." Take your time and remember to listen for – and discuss – solution talk rather than problem talk.

Exercise 5.1
Improving conversations with people you have found difficult in the past

Identify a forthcoming conversation with someone whose conversations you have found difficult to handle previously.

Note their name and the topic of the conversation below:

Despite the difficulties, what can you find that did go well in a previous conversation? Perhaps there was a moment when you asked a useful question, or got an encouraging response? Maybe you were pleased that the person was willing to engage in the conversation with you?

As you look forward to your next conversation with this person, knowing what you now know about constructive conversations, what tactics would you like to try when you speak with them again?

Performance conversations – putting positive difference to work

The next section of the course draws heavily on the work of Gunter Lueger, professor at PEF-University for Management in Vienna, who specialises in developing solutions-focused management instruments.

Constructive conversations about performance at work can make a huge difference to personal and organisational life, impacting on workplace relationships, organisational culture and the bottom-line productivity of the organisation.

The performance conversation or appraisal is an integral part of management, and many organisations rely on this process for making decisions about staffing, defining training needs, providing feedback and setting the direction for future performance. Yet research shows that many people leave performance conversations less motivated than when they went into them.

Often performance reviews take place only once a year, and are structured around some form of rating system where the person is given a number (say between 1-5) or a grade (A, B; or poor, average, good, excellent). It is often assumed that such ratings are a good way of achieving objectives and improving performance.

Yet surveys have shown (Bernardin 1995:464) that:

○ Most of the people who are rated below the highest value on the scale disagree with the rating they are given.
○ A high percentage of those that disagree with the rating they are given are less motivated and less satisfied with their job after the performance review.
○ Most of these dissatisfied people have little or no idea how to improve their performance.

So, using ratings in this way can de-motivate people. It can also lead to conflict. If a manager rates a worker as 'poor' and the worker disagrees, there is immediate friction.

This traditional approach to reviewing performance tends to focus on what has happened in the past. And from that past, little attention is paid to what can be usefully taken from past performance and applied to achieve future results.

One definition of the Solutions Focus approach is "putting positive difference to work". We suggest that by giving people a static rating such as 'poor' or 'good' when talking about their performance over a period of time, you are neglecting variations - significant positive differences that could usefully be put to work.

Take a moment to reflect on your performance at work over the past year. Would you be able to say it was always 'good' or 'excellent' or 'poor' - or would you agree that your performance has fluctuated during the year? Perhaps sometimes it's adequate, at other times excellent, and so on.

These variations can be examined to identify resources, next steps and clues for how to maintain good performance and how to improve over time. When examining the 'positive difference', we are highlighting the times when things went well, when people performed at their best. The skills, resources, behaviours and attributes uncovered here can then be applied to areas where performance is not so good.

This is shown in the diagram below:

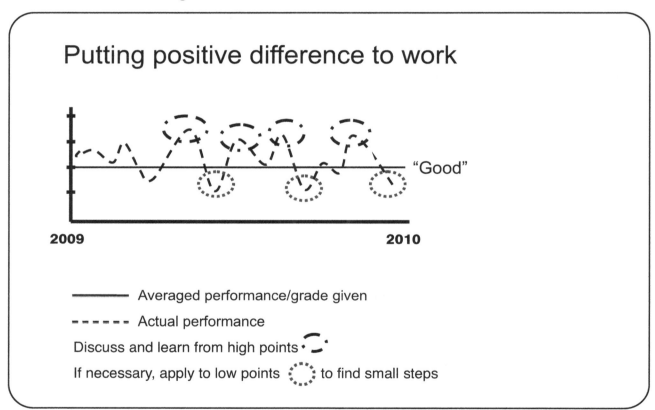

*adapted from G.Lueger, Solutions Focused Rating SFR: New Ways in Performance Appraisal

Gunter Lueger devised the solutions-focused rating system which enables a performance conversation to be more collaborative and engaging by putting these positive differences to work.

His method invites managers to work more constructively while still using their existing performance management forms. A manager could begin, for example, by inviting Helen, the appraised worker, to reflect on her performance over the past year, then to take 100 points and distribute them amongst the existing boxes, which may offer 'Poor, OK, Good and Excellent'.

In the box below, Helen has decided that 40% of her performance over the past year was good, 20% excellent and so on.

Poor	OK	Good	Excellent
10%	30%	40%	20%

There may be a temptation now for Helen's manager to continue the performance conversation by exploring the 'Poor' section. The manager might assume that people will improve their performance most effectively by analysing weaknesses first and attempting to fix them.

But as you will know your work on this course, you are not forced to put your attention on whatever is labelled a weakness. We may instead choose to focus on what we want and on building our strengths to help us achieve this.

Observe the behaviour of Tiger Woods, hailed as the greatest golfer of our time. In 2002, Woods was rated number one in the world on 'Green in Regulation' shots, the measure of how many shots you are expected to play before getting your ball onto the green. He was also rated 62nd in the world at 'Sand Saves', your history of getting out of a bunker and into the hole in two shots (or better).

Woods could have chosen to focus on his perceived weakness and practice his sand saves. Instead he worked on his swing until it was so strong and predictable he would land on the green and not in the sand. He didn't attempt directly to improve his sand saves. In 2007 Woods was still leading the world ranking in golf – and he had slipped down to number 83 in the ranking for Sand Saves. Here Woods made his weaknesses irrelevant by developing his strengths.

Picking up on this idea of working on strengths, the SF performance conversation begins by exploring the 'Excellent' category, with the manager asking resource-based questions to elicit detail of achievements and top performance, to provide clues and motivation for further such attainment.

In this conversation, (as with Scaling), we:
○ Accept the person's rating
○ Ask about what worked in each instance
○ Collect Counters
○ Give Affirms and amplify resources.

Once we have exhausted 'Excellent', we can move onto 'Good'. By the time the conversation has reaches 'Poor', we shall have a better sense of how much time, if any, to devote to discussing improvement in this area. If we choose to do so, it is now on a basis of a rich selection of resources, Counters and success stories. As with Tiger Woods, it may make more sense to grow a worker's strengths than to try to fix their 'weaknesses'.

These will be more collaborative conversations focusing on agreed good performance – with ratings unchallenged by the appraiser – and discussion centred on how to sustain what's going well and identify further opportunities for progress.

The table below shows some of the differences between this approach and the traditional approach to performance interviews:

Traditional approach in appraisal interview	Solutions-orientated approach in appraisal interview
Standardised approach to the process	Flexible application which can fit each person
Goal setting, if any, is vague	Precise description of what is wanted
Concentration on the person's deficits and weaknesses	Discussion of strengths and successes and starting points for improvements
Tendency to make the person fit the job	Possibility of adapting the job to fit with the person's strengths
Discussion of failures in the past	Future and goal-orientated
Raters make suggestions as to what the person should do	Rater and person being rated work out the changes together
High expectations of performance conversations: Ideally all problems will be solved and major progress made	Concentration on small feasible steps that encourage change
Appreciation- if present at all – is a tool and not an attitude	Appreciation as an attitude is palpable in the discussion of common, every-day success
Average performance can lose useful distinctions	Highlights useful differences in performance - 'putting positive difference to work'

Adapted from G.Lueger, Solutions Focused Rating SFR: New Ways in Performance Appraisal

Exercise 5.2
Review your own performance

Now it's your turn to have a go.

Think about your performance at work over the past three months or so.

Award yourself 100 points spread over these categories:

Poor	OK	Good	Excellent

Starting with **Excellent**

When was this?

What about it made it Excellent?

What specifically did you do well here?

What might others have noticed about you when you were being excellent?

What else is it useful for you to notice here?

Moving onto **Good**

When was your performance good?

What was happening when it was good?

What were you specifically contributing that made it good?

What would your boss, colleagues, customers say they noticed about you when your performance was good?

What else is it useful for you to notice here?

OK

When was your performance OK - be specific?

What were the highlights of OK for you?

What else is useful for you to notice here?

Affirming

Take a moment to reflect on what you've noted about your excellent, good and OK performance.

List the resources this has highlighted, skills you have that you would like to continue using and to amplify.

What else might be useful for you as you now move onto improving your performance in the future?

(If time), Poor

Where was your performance poor?

Reflecting on all the resources, skills and attributes you've uncovered from the previous sections:

Which - if any - of these areas is it important to improve?

Make a note of the resources you could use to improve performance here:

Small Actions

Given what you're hoping to achieve in the next three months…

Jot down some small actions or things that are useful for you to notice which will enable you to make progress.

You can apply Solutions-focused Rating to many popular assessment tools. For example, 360-degree evaluation processes typically assess people's competencies on a scale of 1-5 from the perspective of the line manager, the person being assessed and their direct reports. Taking a solutions-focused approach to a discussion of the results would involve first exploring the competencies where people scored well rather than the areas where they scored low.

We have worked with a number of UK-based Further Education colleges over the years. The colleges are inspected by the governing body, OFSTED, which measures quality and performance on a scale of 1-4, (1 being outstanding and 4 meaning failing). Teachers' performance is also measured against this scale. It is essential that colleges score 3 and above over all, or they are classified as a 'failing college' and special measures are applied.

We worked with an Inner London college for a number of years, introducing solutions-focused tools and techniques to the managers and then the teachers. The college had a problem with low-performing teachers who continually received 4's in their assessments.

The college managers applied the solutions-focused rating system to their lesson observations, and over time, by changing the kind of conversations they had, review grades started to rise. Those being assessed said that it was the first time they had been asked about what they were doing well, and that by building on this it was far easier for them to improve their performance. They reported that the old evaluation system had simply told them how poor their performance was, leaving them with no idea how to improve and little motivation to do so.

As you can see, this kind of rating can be used in any conversation concerned with reviewing and improving performance, such as:

❍ A manager reviewing the performance of a direct report
❍ A coach and client discussing the client's progress
❍ A project team discussing how they are performing against the project plan
❍ A teacher and child reviewing the child's progress or behaviour in class over a given time period
❍ A consultant evaluating a project with a client.

Tools review & memory prompts

When you're changing conversations you might like some prompts to help you remember important points, making the most of the tips and techniques available from each tool. Here's how to create such prompts.

Exercise 5.3
Making your cards

Looking back over the previous chapters and remembering what has been useful and interesting for you, create a set of cards which will act as memory prompts for each tool. One tool per card for:

Platform
Future Perfect
Scaling
Counters
Affirm
Small Actions

On these cards write down the most important elements and key questions.

You might also draw pictures and symbols that will remind you of how best to apply each tool.

You may create other cards, such as a 'What else?' card, or one with the Solutions Strategy model on it – these are prompts for your own conversations, so decide what's going to be most useful for you.

Now you have these cards you can refer to them when appropriate. Some of our colleagues have placed them on notice boards in their offices; others carry them around and pull them out just before or even during a conversation.

JAM Sessions – 'Just A Minute' conversations

As well as responding in the moment by asking that incisive question or noticing a key resource to affirm, we can also prepare sets of questions for certain types of recurring situations.

Constructive conversations don't always need to be in-depth, long or scheduled. You may also notice that there are themes to your conversations. One manager we worked with was continually being asked to help his staff prepare for their difficult conversations with team members; another found that people often came to her asking for help when preparing for interviews.

Perhaps you regularly need to prepare for meetings, or need to make quick decisions, and would get benefits from having a tailored set of questions to ask yourself each time.

For these occasions we use JAM (Just A Minute) Sessions, so-named by Jackie Keddy of The Metropolitan Police, who based them in turn on the pioneering work of Michael Hjerth, a Swedish-based solutions-focused trainer and consultant, who calls them micro-tools.

The idea is to create short and concise lists of questions related to a specific topic that you can use yourself and with your colleagues.

Criteria for creating JAM sessions

JAM sessions should:

○ Fit with a specific situation, eg meetings, presentations, making decisions
○ Use some or all of the solutions-focused tools
○ Take no longer than 5 minutes to work through
○ Consist of 4-8 questions
○ Be self-contained and self-instructing

Here's an example of a JAM session

Preparing for a meeting

❍ What is your task in this meeting?

❍ What is your purpose?

❍ What would you like to see happen as a result of this meeting?

❍ What is the least you would like to see happen?

❍ What have you done previously to achieve this kind of thing?

❍ What can you do now?

❍ What is your first step?

* adapted from micro-tool developed by Michael Hjerth

Exercise 5.4
Now it's your turn to work through the JAM session

Answer the questions in relation to a meeting you would like to prepare for:

What is your task in this meeting?

What is your purpose? What would you like to see happen as a result of this meeting?

What is the least you would like to see happen?

What have you done previously to achieve this kind of thing?

What can you do now?

What is your first step?

How was that useful?

Now find a colleague or friend to try this out with and ask them how it was useful for them. Note their comments below.

Here's another JAM session we developed that you may like to try:

Preparing for a tricky conversation

○ What are your best hopes for this conversation?

○ What do you both want?

○ What do you value about this person?

○ What's worked well in the past in similar situations?

○ What will be the first signs that things are going well?

○ What else might be useful here?

○ What can you do now and/or in the meeting?

Exercise 5.5
Creating your own JAM sessions

Note the topics for which you consider it would be useful to have JAM sessions. These can be topics you would find helpful for yourself and those that are relevant to the people you work and spend your days with. One example might be preparing for presentations.

Now choose from these topics the one that would be most useful for you to develop into a JAM session. Write your JAM session, remembering to follow these guidelines:

- ○ Fit with a specific situation
- ○ Uses some or all of SF tools
- ○ 5 minutes long
- ○ 4-8 questions
- ○ Should be self-contained & self-instructing

Title..

Try this out on yourself and your colleagues.

Having tried it, what changes or improvements could you make?

Note anything else that would be helpful for you in relation to developing and using JAM sessions.

Summary of the main points of week 5

○ In this chapter we have expanded our tool kit by exploring how best to follow up a conversation; applied tools to generate more constructive performance conversations; developed memory prompts and JAM sessions. Notice that you now have an extensive and flexible tool kit that can be applied to any topic or situation you would like to make progress with.

○ Change can take place over a number of conversations. Be prepared to follow-up your initial conversations, starting by exploring 'What's better?'

○ Solutions-focused Rating will allow you to 'put positive differences to work'. By using this rating system, you can have collaborative, constructive and motivational discussions about performance with your direct reports, your manager, colleagues and customers.

○ You can have a 5-minute conversation that makes a significant difference. Create and use your JAM sessions and notice how people respond.

References and further reading for this week

Lueger G: Solutions Focused Rating SFR: New Ways in Performance Appraisal: Solutions Focused Management, Lueger + Korn, 2006.

Plenary Presentation by Hjerth M: Solutions Focus in organisations, Cologne 2008

Plenary Presentation by Buckingham M: Appreciative Inquiry Conference, Orlando November 2007.

Week 6: Keeping the conversation going

In this final week, we reflect on your learning so far, then explore how you might take further steps to increase your prospects of even more constructive conversations. We present a handy table that may help you quickly find a suitable style for a greater range of conversations. In particular, we examine how to deal with difficult questions, when for example facing an audience during a meeting or presentation. Then we dive into the word-by-word details of conversation - the realm of micro-language and a reminder of pre-suppositions.

Our work on constructive conversations can be placed within the wider context of a growing movement featuring a variety of positive approaches to change; and we take a look at that intellectual landscape too.

Sometimes positively speaking is a matter of confidence as much as technique, and we can draw on our knowledge of an interactional world to ensure that we retain sufficient confidence as a dialogue develops.

Reflection on learning

Take a moment to reflect on what you have discovered during the weeks of this study guide. Where have you used the tools and ideas effectively? What other tips and techniques have you found that work for you?

Which conversations do you find it relatively easy to make constructive? Which conversations are still more of a struggle?

Check your progress below by completing the same questionnaire that we met in the first chapter and comparing your results.

Exercise 6.1
Benchmarking

Remember at the start of this study guide you created a benchmark for your current skills in holding constructive conversations. Find the answers from that chart on page 129 and compare where you are now on each scale.

Rate yourself on a scale of 1 (lowest) to 10 (highest) on each of the following:

I am consistently successful in persuading people what to do

I am good at handling my own strong emotions in conversations

I am good at handling other people's strong emotions during conversations

I prepare well for difficult conversations

I am good at staying polite when provoked

You may also have added further statements that described how you would like to be in relation to your constructive conversations – and then rated yourself against the scale. How have you progressed with these?

Where have you made most progress?

How did you do that?

What does that tell you about your strengths, skills and resources in this area?

Where would you like to put your attention now?

Increasing your range

We know that conversations are infinitely variable and no one model is likely to cover every situation. Here's a useful table for helping to stretch the range of constructive conversations with which you can be comfortable. Like any model, it has limitations and the most important aspect remains your individual skill in judging what is appropriate and responding improvisationally during the conversation as it unfolds.

Situation Conditions	Communications Style
The issue is open to rational debate You are seen as a technical expert You can draw on facts and examples	Give the facts as they become relevant. Remember that turn-taking is often important to keep the dialogue going.
You are clear about what you want You'd like the other person to understand your needs	State your objectives. Allow each participant to say what they want, then invite summaries of the needs.
You don't know the person's position You want to show support and encouragement	Ask questions and encourage contributions – affirming and thanking.
You want to build trust in the relationship The other person sees you as a threat	Disclose something about yourself – a personal story or detail. Take time to listen.
It is important to generate excitement Your vision might appeal to the other person	Discuss benefits. Describe the Future Perfect.
A new problem has arisen It's the first time you've worked with the other person	Start with problem-free talk, to get resourceful. What are they interested in?
Information about advantages and disadvantages would help clarify the choices There are positive and negative consequences to not meeting your demands You need the issue resolved	Keep the conversation to a time limit or deadline. Discuss the consequences of each possible path.
You are dealing with an emotive topic You feel strongly about the issue You need to add weight to your basic assertion	Stay calm. It's OK to describe how you are feeling. Remain assertive, not aggressive.

Dealing with difficult questions

Here is a routine we developed for dealing with difficult questions. This can apply in circumstances ranging from a conventional one-to-one conversation - when you suddenly feel the force of an emotional question or challenge - to a formal presentation - when you need to answer a question from a member of the audience while still retaining the interest of the audience as a whole.

The format or pattern is CEA:

○ Clarify
○ Emotion
○ Answer

The temptation when facing a challenging or provocative question is to dive straight into your answer: "Here's what I think…." which may of course sometimes work. But often you can make more of the opportunity that such a question provides, by dealing with the emotional force that underpins the question itself.

First, we clarify.
>*So you are asking about my reasons for deciding to leave now.*
>*You are saying that you disapprove of the ban on hunting…*
>*The question is about who decides where we will build the new classrooms.*

This may involve repeating the question word-for-word, which shows that you have at least been listening carefully. Or it may be that a summary is more appropriate – helping to shape a question into manageable form.

Then we address the emotional component – giving it its due, connecting with the questioner on the emotional level:
>*You sound pretty angry about this.*
>*I guess that you are puzzled by my statement.*
>*Many people are curious when I propose this..*

Take a moment to notice if you have made an emotional connection. A nod, or a short 'yes', gives you the cue to move on to the Answer:

> *Well, what I mean is…*
> *Yes, there will be cutbacks in our staffing for this project.*
> *We clearly have different views about this topic. Here's my reasoning…*

If you are using this CEA format with an audience, it helps to address the Clarify part to the entire audience:

> *"This is a question about the details of the rollout of the new initiative – which will involve all of your teams."*

You can see to what extent everyone's interest is engaged, and decide how much time to devote to the answer. It may be better to answer the question later to only the questioner or to a smaller group that really wants to know.

The Emotion element can be directed most effectively to the person who asks the question:

> *It sounds like you have strong views about this.*
> *I was angry too when I learned the truth.*

Sometimes the questioner is more concerned to know they have been heard and understood than they are to hear the 'rational' answer to the words of their question. This emotional beat also gives them the opportunity to correct any misunderstanding:

> *No, it's more that I was surprised when you first said it. Actually, it's fine.*
> *That's right – I'm furious and I demand to know precisely who authorised this.*

Finally, you give the Answer to the whole group, on the assumption that everyone is interested or will need to know. Keep the Answer brief.

Exercise 6.2
Responding to challenging questions

This is an exercise for you to do with a partner or a group of people.

One of you is the speaker; the role of the other(s) is to ask challenging questions. The speaker begins by giving an improvised, impromptu talk for about one minute on any subject of their choice. It can be any topic – recommended ways to improve the country's transport system; why hedgehogs should be shot on sight; the need to grow our own starch. The speaker is assumed to be the expert in the topic, however ridiculous.

The speaker concludes after the minute and invites questions.

The audience ask a series of questions – challenging, pertinent, technical, rambling.

The speaker deals with the questions using the CEA format.

You can of course then swap roles.

To debrief, discuss:

To what extent did the CEA format help the speaker to handle the questions?

What variations to the format are helpful in particular circumstances?

Micro-language

It is said that the devil is in the detail, meaning in our case that we can usefully examine the smallest fractions of communication. That is precisely the work that's been undertaken by researchers such as Paul Watzlawick, Don Jackson and particularly Janet Bavelas.

The researchers record a chunk of a conversation – say a five-minute section of a therapist talking to client, or teacher to a child – and transcribe it, including lengths of pauses, and all the 'ah-has', 'mm's and other vocal noises.

Each person's contribution or the conversation as a whole can then be analysed – usually against pre-determined criteria. For example, the research team might agree on what constitute respectively positive and negative interventions, so that one speaker may be compared with another.

It's even possible to take such a test yourself, which is what students of solution focused brief therapy (SFBT) do within the Tri-Phase Microanalysis approach to teaching solution-building skills to helping professionals under the guidance of Professor Ron Warner at the University of Toronto.

This Tri-Phase approach is illustrated in his recent book, Solution-Focused Interviewing: A Tri-Phase Approach to Using Strength-Based Questions Within a Positive Psychology Framework.

This approach includes checking your own and others conversations against the following criteria:

○ To what extent do you think your conversations would rate as constructive or solutions-oriented?
○ Do you avoid the pitfalls of getting drawn into problem-talk, analysing and investigating problems?
○ Do you stay on the solutions track of finding out what people want, what resources they have for getting it and what actions might be useful in making progress?

Here's an example of a choice of question at this micro level. Steve de Shazer began his interview with a therapeutic client, as he typically would, by asking how the client spent his day. The client, who had been referred for therapy because of his problem drinking, said, "I spend my day drinking and listening to music." De Shazer responded, "What sort of music?" – as neat an illustration as you could wish of avoiding the temptation to switch to the problem axis.

Any emphasis on micro-analysis will remind you of the reading in Week 3 about pre-suppositional language. It's the opportunity to build in your assumptions question by question: instead of saying, "Will you ever get that homework finished?", you can assume the goodwill and practical skills of the child, and ask, "When will you be getting that homework finished?"

Similarly, if people you are speaking to are clearly struggling with a problem, you can include statements to normalise their difficulties:

Many people would find this difficult.
I remember having a lot of trouble with this myself.
It's not unusual for this to be tricky at first...

Asking questions

In many constructive conversations you will find yourself asking questions – a natural enough device for eliciting the information you want. Questions need to be used with care. There's a risk that your conversational partners might experience questions as aggressive. This is particularly likely if you use 'Why?' questions, as they prompt the response 'Because' – with its implications of justification and even defensiveness. A 'why?' question also sets off a search for a reason where there may be no single explicable reason (it's a complex world). Writing about questions in their book Children's Solution Work, Insoo Kim Berg and Therese Steiner comment that questions such as 'How would that be helpful to you?' and 'What difference would it make between the two of you?' tend to be more helpful than 'why?' questions in finding out more about what people want. Try this out with a colleague. Invite them to tell you about a recent experience and then only ask them questions beginning with 'Why?' Notice where this takes the conversation. Now start the conversation over, this time asking 'How?' or 'What?' questions. What do you notice is different in the responses? Why?

Conversations for outstanding results

In one sense constructive conversations are 'just talk'. But talk can be tremendously powerful. Your conversations may generate creative ideas that change people's lives and redirect the world. Conversations are the foundation of therapeutic work, coaching relationships and collaboration in every aspect of life.

Of course you don't need to be a 'professional' to hold constructive conversations.

Yet professionals can reap the interactive bonuses of their professional contexts: your credibility in the eyes of your conversational partners makes a difference, as does the 'title' given to the conversational setting. The same words are not the same conversation if they take place as a 'therapy session' or as a 'water-cooler chat'.

In his book, American Therapy - The Rise of Psychotherapy in the United States, Jonathan Engel describes an experiment by Vanderbilt University researcher Hans Strupp in 1979. He divided 30 patients with psychological problems into two groups; one group was treated by trained psychotherapists, the other by humanities professors with no psychological expertise. Each group reported improvement at the same rates. Engel writes, "Effective psychotherapy seemed to require little more than a willing patient and an intelligent and understanding counselor who met and spoke regularly and in confidence."

What are the principal ways to ensure outstanding results from your conversations? One simple method is to do more to choose when to have the conversations that count – and when not to.

The more resourceful you feel, the better your conversations are likely to turn out. Hold them at times when you are feeling fresh, alert and energised. Sometimes it is possible to reschedule to a more auspicious time. You can also choose times when your partners will be feeling more receptive, creative or collaborative – depending on which aspects of their resources you wish to engage.

Hold your talks in places where you feel comfortable, confident and relaxed. Choose locations that work well for you and invite your conversational partners to join you there.

If a conversation does take a turn for the worse and is worth saving, perhaps you can call for a time out. Suggest that you reconvene later or elsewhere to continue the conversation. Apologise for the break or the delay, then get out without saying anything you'll regret.

An interactional circle of confidence

Once you have mastered the various techniques presented in this study guide, the remaining element that enables you to have fully constructive conversations is the confidence to apply those techniques.

When that is the case, it can help to be aware of the confidence circle, a practical illustration of the solution-focused principle of Inbetween – the action is in the interaction. Another way of looking at it is to say 'confidence' isn't something you simply 'have' (or don't have), it is something you do in relation to other people.

Let's suppose you are about to begin a conversation with another person. There is a moment at which that person sees you – perhaps as you enter the room. You will be moving at a certain speed, exuding a degree of energy, with a particular expression on your face.

Your conversational partner can (and will) make all sorts of judgements about you at that moment, and – if asked – would be able to rate your level of confidence on a scale of 1 to 10. They can do this almost instantly and the judgement they make will affect their response to you.

If you appear to be confident, they are likely to have confidence in you. Imagine, for example, you are a nurse who has come in to give an injection to a patient. By moving steadily, directly, smiling and making eye contact with the patient, you appear confident. The patient immediately starts to trust you, believing in your competence. (They don't know it's your first day, and you've never done this before).

Conversely, by entering timidly and looking anxious, you undermine their confidence in you, increasing whatever nervousness they are already experiencing. In the first instance, you have set up a virtuous circle – in which their confidence sustains your confidence. In the second, a vicious circle, in which each fumble and shake leads to further lack of trust in each other. Notice that these interactional circles of response depend primarily on how you appear to each other at the moment of first noticing – not on how you felt when you came into the room. You may feel almost anything, yet present yourself in whatever way you wish. It's what actors do when they are on stage, and it could be considered part of the professional duty of anyone who works in a context in which there may be benefits from that professional appearing confident.

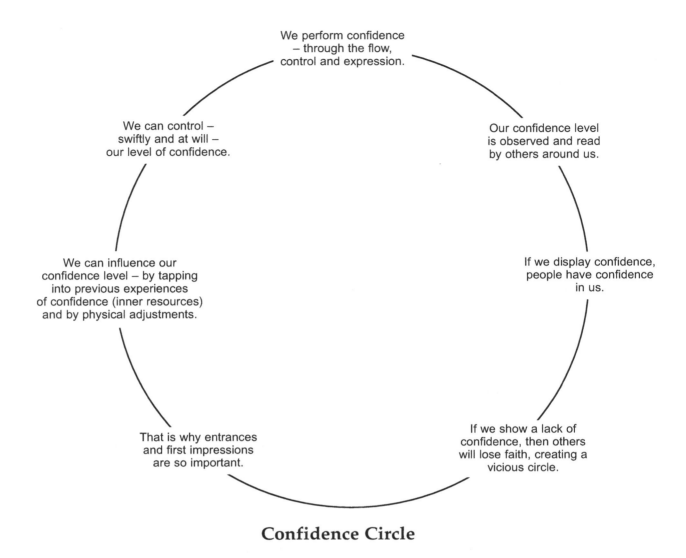

We perform confidence
– through the flow,
control and expression.

We can control –
swiftly and at will –
our level of confidence.

Our confidence level
is observed and read
by others around us.

We can influence our
confidence level – by tapping
into previous experiences
of confidence (inner resources)
and by physical adjustments.

If we display confidence,
people have confidence
in us.

That is why entrances
and first impressions
are so important.

If we show a lack of
confidence, then others
will lose faith, creating a
vicious circle.

Confidence Circle

Displaying confidence to engender further confidence can be the key to creating a constructive conversation. It's part of the contextual, interactional mix that allows your conversational partners to find and express their resourcefulness, encouraging you to further bring your resourcefulness to the enterprise.

Context is construction

How is it that mere conversations can make so much difference? We think that the constructionist view of the world offers a persuasive account.

Our very identities are constructed in interaction with everything around us – including (perhaps most significantly) other people. This offers a different way of thinking about ourselves from the prevalent "obvious" view of ourselves as individuals.

People's own, individualistic accounts of themselves are notoriously unreliable. What they tell researchers, for example, about their own behaviour is often plain wrong. They will tell you, naturally enough, that they eat as much as they want, for example, and won't be influenced by the packaging. Yet food psychologists have discovered that people eat more of a product if it comes in a bigger package. They drink more than a third more fruit juice when they pour it into a short, wide glass instead of a narrow, tall one.

In these cases what they are doing is not dependent primarily on hunger or thirst, or what kind of people they are (or think they are) – not on what might be seen as 'inner states' – but on contextual elements that create particular types of interaction with them.

> *Staying with the food psychologists, we learn that people will report that a breakfast bar tastes worse if the packaging describes it as containing soy, even if it contains no soy, and that Black Forest Double-Chocolate Cake tastes better than Chocolate Cake, even when the cakes themselves are identical.*
>
> (Guardian newspaper 23.08.06)

> *It may seem obvious that cyclists can be safer if they wear helmets. But that is to take an individual rather than interactional view. Our Guardian newspaper reports research that motorists will be more careful about driving a safe distance from a cyclist if the cyclist is not wearing a helmet. Neither cyclists nor drivers operate in isolation – there is a dynamic system on the road, and it is at that level that we might most usefully consider safety.*
>
> (Cycling safety… Guardian 11.08.08)

And so it is with conversations. Words alone can perturb the system to make differences to how people think, feel and act – adjusting their performance in often surprising directions. A short conversation before a maths exam can impact how well students perform: girls subtly reminded they were female scored lower on their exam than those who were reminded they were privileged (to be at a certain school). (Washington Post.) These are examples of what psychologists call 'priming' effects – whereby things said or done before the actual event in question affect performance. We can think of constructive conversations as careful cultivation of priming, preparing people to perform at their best in the forthcoming tasks.

Conversation as a positive approach

We see our ideas of constructive conversations as part of the current wave of positive approaches to change that you can find in a range of disciplines, from psychology to organisational development.

We would include:

Positive psychology, which offers a research base that provides a great deal of empirical support for the use of the tools and principles outlined in this study guide.

The body of work of solution-focused brief therapists (SFBT), who built their practice case by case by noticing what worked, making progressive adjustments to their methods as they reviewed video and audio tapes of their conversations with clients.

Appreciative Inquiry, an approach to organisational interventions, originally associated with academics at Case Western University, initiated by David Cooperrider and Suresh Srivastva in 1980, then spreading around the world over several decades into large companies, communities and supra-governmental institutions with encouraging results.

The Strengths movement, based on Gallop polls of large numbers of respondents, which indicates that paying attention to top performers and personal strengths can give individuals, teams and organisations a cutting edge. As Robert Biswas- Diener reports in the study guide, Invitation to Positive Psychology, "The best managers showed that they emphasised strengths over seniority in making personnel decisions, had a tendency to match talents with tasks, and spent more time with their top producers." (Week 4). Organisations that encourage their workers to use their strengths tend to flourish as these workers become more engaged.

We have previously mentioned solution focused brief therapy (SFBT) and the work of Steve de Shazer and Insoo Kim Berg as primary sources of our approach. Other contemporary approaches to therapy and consultation that generate enriching conversations include Narrative Therapy and Collaborative Therapy. Narrative Therapy constructs and explores enriching stories, discovering "unique outcomes" from the past which can make a positive difference in telling new stories about ourselves. Collaborative therapy emphasizes a philosophical stance or way of "being with" the other person that invites generative dialogues.

Inspired by SFBT, there's now a growing network of Solutions Focus applications, centred especially on the members of the SOL network, a worldwide community of practitioners who share case studies and ideas in an ever-increasing range of applications, including strategic work in organisations, coaching, negotiating and team-building.

There are regular conferences at which you can meet and discuss work with other practitioners who are developing this fascinating field; and several well-stocked websites from which to gather resources and join in on-line discussions. We list some of these at the end of this chapter.

Naturally, each practitioner or group of practitioners will have their own particular emphasis on what matters most or what makes most difference, but they all shelter under a broad umbrella that holds that conversation can be the catalyst for nurturing change, prompting fresh creativity and enabling people to make progress.

In societies which value, reward and celebrate individual achievement, perhaps too little credit is given to the power of conversation in enabling any individual to claim their dues. It might be tempting, when faced with someone successful, to ask, "Who have you been talking to?", if only so that a significant part of such stories is not neglected.

In his book "Infinite Potential" F. David Peat reports physicist David Bohm appreciating that conversations made significant contributions to the development of his ideas: (page 154) "After Yevick and Vigier departed, Bohm was struck by the realization that, "I depend much more then I thought on such conversation, in order to bring out dormant ideas into a definite form, and to prevent them from continuing to "sleep" forever...."

The great British football manager, Brian Clough, who guided two provincial teams to the League Championship and twice won the European Cup, was famed for unorthodox methods of motivating his players, and a comparative neglect of fancy tactical systems. He said, "It only takes a minute to score a goal, and it takes less than a minute to change someone's outlook with a word or two. That's just another form of coaching which you won't find in the manuals."

Provided You Don't Kiss Me, by Duncan Hamilton.

Another story in the same book reminds us of Ludwig Wittgenstein's remark that we learn by re-arranging what we know. The revered comedians Morecambe and Wise had a sketch in which piano playing Eric Morecambe is challenged by conductor Andre Previn, "You're playing all the wrong notes." Eric responds, "I'm playing all the right notes but not necessarily in the right order."

Commenting on the sketch, Clough adds, "The difference between a good manager and a bad one is that a good one (a) can recognise they can play and (b) knows how to teach them to put everything in the right order."

What to do and what not to do

William James said, "The art of being wise is knowing what to overlook." More recently (op cit p) Berg and Steiner wrote, "Successful parenting requires parents to be selectively deaf, blind and mute."

In this course we have learnt a great deal about what to do. The converse is always a whole range of 'what not to do's'. We have sometimes made these explicit – as in the advice to resist Problem Talk. At other times the 'what not to do's' are implicit, partly because it would be tedious to list all the ways we get drawn off the track of constructive conversation and partly because every conversation offers infinite opportunities to become less constructive.

Nonetheless – despite all the temptations and natural inclinations to be less than constructive - it remains possible to build your own skills and the skills of other people to enjoy and benefit from constructive conversations. A wrong turn in any conversation need not be fatal – conversation is a forgiving medium, in which it is generally possible to have another go to get things back on track as the dialogue continues.

Summary of the main points of week 6

○ You have checked your progress since starting this study guide.

○ You can broaden your range of responses, partly by planning and recognising a variety of circumstances, partly by improvising skilfully in the moment.

○ Handle questions by using the format Clarify – Emotion – Answer.

○ You can fruitfully examine conversation at the micro level, word by word; and at the highest levels of context – the credibility of your setting and all the interactional factors that influence how people respond to each other.

○ One key interactional factor is the exercise of confidence to generate further confidence.

○ Constructive conversations are part of the positive approaches to change that are showing great results in a variety of fields – and there are growing communities to develop and support such approaches.

○ As you build your expertise, be aware of what you do – and also what you don't do.

References and further reading for this week

Jackson PZ & McKergow M: The Solutions Focus – Making Coaching & Change SIMPLE. Nicholas Brealey International 2007. chapter 15

Engel J: American Therapy,The Rise of Psychotherapy in the United States, Gotham Books. 2008.

Watzlawick P, Bavelas J & Jackson D: Pragmatics of Human Communication, New York, Norton. 1967

For the work of Janet Bavelas and colleagues - http://web.uvic.ca/psyc/bavelas/Communication.html

Bavelas JB, McGee D, Phillips B & Routledge R: (2000). Microanalysis of communication in psychotherapy. *Human Systems, 11*, 47-66. [Actually appeared in 2002]. Translated into Spanish and reprinted (2003): *Sistemas Famililares, 19*, 23-41.

McGee D R, Del Vento A, & Bavelas J B: (2004/2005). An interactional model of questions as therapeutic interventions. Simultaneous publication in *Journal of Marital and Family Therapy* (2005, *31*, 371-384) and *Sistemas Familiares* (2004, *20*, 51-66).

Tomori C & Bavelas J: (Accepted for publication). Using microanalysis of communication to compare solution-focused and client-centered therapies. *Journal of Family Psychotherapy.*

Warner Dr. RE: Solution-Focused Interviewing: A Tri-Phase Approach to Using Strength-Based Questions Within a Positive Psychology Framework, Raven Press. 2005: "Assessing Solution-Building Skills: A Tri-Phase Microanalysis Approach".

A presentation at the third annual Solution-Focused Brief Therapy Association in Fort Lauderdale, Florida.

Berg IK & Steiner T: Children's Solution Work, Norton, 2003.

Hamilton D: Provided You Don't Kiss Me, Fourth Estate Ltd, 2008

Biswas-Diener R: Invitation to Positive Psychology, Capp Press, UK, 2008

Internet resources

Collaborative Practices

http://www.harlene.org

http://www.talkhgi.com

http://www.california.com/~rathbone/pmth.htm

NarrativePractices

http://www.dulwichcentre.com.au

http://www.eftc.org

http://www.narrativeapproaches.com

Solution-Focused Therapy

http://www.brief-therapy.org

http://www.brieftherapy.org.uk

Further study opportunities

If you have enjoyed this study guide and want to learn more with us, please get in touch to find details of our open courses and in-house training courses. It is also possible for organisations to licence our materials for their own use.

You can contact us at:

Web: www.thesolutionsfocus.co.uk

Email: contact@thesolutionsfocus.co.uk

Phone: +44 (0) 1727 840 340

Our programs include:

Coaching with a Solutions Focus

Team Coaching with a Solutions Focus

Solutions Focus Professional

Introduction to Solutions Focus

Solutions Focused Leadership

Constructive Conversations

Team building and development

Strategic Planning Sessions

Managing for great performance

Solutions Focused 360° feedback

License packs include:

Full timetable guide

Pack of activities

Poster Set

Slides

DVD clip recommendations

Participant booklet

Trainer guide

Solutions at Work CD

About the authors

PAUL Z JACKSON and JANINE WALDMAN are co-directors of coaching and change consultancy The Solutions Focus. Based in St Albans UK, they lead an experienced team of consultants, facilitators and coaches who apply this approach worldwide.

PAUL Z JACKSON is an inspirational consultant and coach, who devises and runs training courses and development programs in strategy, leadership, teamwork, creativity and innovation.

His expertise in the solutions focus approach, improvisation and accelerated learning has attracted corporate clients and public organisations, ranging from Cranfield Business School to Procter & Gamble, from local authorities to top five accountants and leading campaign groups.

Previously a journalist, senior producer with BBC Radio and director of the *More Fool Us* improvisation comedy team, he is a graduate of Oxford University and his books include *Impro Learning, 58½ Ways to Improvise in Training, The Inspirational Trainer* and (as co-author) *The Solutions Focus* and *Positively Speaking*.

Co-founder of both *SOLworld* and the *Applied Improvisation Network* (of which he is President), Paul is a popular keynote speaker and workshop presenter at conferences around the world.

JANINE WALDMAN has almost two decades of experience in her specialisms of executive coaching and training, as well as a wealth of expertise in consultancy and organisational development, having held senior HR positions in both the UK and New Zealand prior to becoming co-director of The Solutions Focus.

A graduate of The London School of Economics, she holds a masters degree in Industrial Relations and Human Resource Management. She is a welcome and frequent presenter at international conferences on solutions-focused approaches. A Fellow of the CIPD, she is a Visiting Lecturer on HRM and strategy, and lectures on post-graduate courses, both at Birkbeck and Westminster Universities.

Janine has a dynamic international coaching practice and specialises in working with organisations to bring about positive change and implementing constructive and resourceful ways of working. She has trained numerous managers and coaches in solutions-focused approaches worldwide, working with a plethora of private and public sector organisations. Her prestigious client base includes: London Metropolitan Police, Bieresdorf AG (Nivea), Ashridge Business School, Reading Borough Council and John Laing.

Lightning Source UK Ltd.
Milton Keynes UK
UKOW07f1334150615

253505UK00013B/339/P

9 780956 526908